Liminality in Organization Studies

In a time of flexible and mutable work arrangements, there is hardly a domain of organizing that has not been affected by liminality. Temporary workers who switch companies based on projects, consultants who operate at the boundaries between the consultant and the client companies, or 'hybrid entrepreneurs' who start new ventures, while still keeping their previous job, are examples of liminality in organizations. Liminality is also felt by managers who handle interorganizational relationships within customer-supplier networks or scientists who, albeit affiliated with R&D units, have strong ties with their scientific communities, acknowledging that they belong to neither setting thoroughly. Precious hints for enriching our comprehension of liminality in organizational settings can be conveyed by the reflection that has flourished in different fields.

This book advances knowledge of liminality management by elaborating on a model that puts together aspects of the liminal process that have been mostly described in a separate way so far, benefiting from the input provided by experience in sociology, medicine, and education. Through the articulation of a model that accounts for the antecedents, content, and consequences of liminality in organizations, the book intends to prompt quantitative research on this topic. It will be of value to those interested in organizational behavior, organization and management, marketing, sociology of work, and sociology of organizations.

Maria Rita Tagliaventi is an Associate Professor of Organizational Behavior at the University of Bologna, Italy.

Routledge Focus on Business and Management

The fields of business and management have grown exponentially as areas of research and education. This growth presents challenges for readers trying to keep up with the latest important insights. Routledge Focus on Business and Management presents small books on big topics and how they intersect with the world of business research.

Individually, each title in the series provides coverage of a key academic topic, whilst collectively, the series forms a comprehensive collection across the business disciplines.

Heidegger and Entrepreneurship
A Phenomenological Approach
Håvard Åsvoll

The Politics of Organizational Change
Robert Price

Globalization and Entrepreneurship in Small Countries
Mirjana Radović-Marković and Rajko Tomaš

The Business of New Process Diffusion
Management of the Early Float Glass Start-ups
Brychan Celfyn Thomas and Alun Merlyn Thomas

Liminality in Organization Studies
Theory and Method
Maria Rita Tagliaventi

For more information about this series, please visit: www.routledge.com/Routledge-Focus-on-Business-and-Management/book-series/FBM

Liminality in Organization Studies

Theory and Method

Maria Rita Tagliaventi

Routledge
Taylor & Francis Group

NEW YORK AND LONDON

First published 2020
by Routledge
52 Vanderbilt Avenue, New York, NY 10017

and by Routledge
2 Park Square, Milton Park, Abingdon, Oxon, OX14 4RN

Routledge is an imprint of the Taylor & Francis Group, an informa business

Library of Congress Cataloging-in-Publication Data
Names: Tagliaventi, Maria Rita, author.
Title: Liminality in organization studies: theory and
method / Maria Rita Tagliaventi.
Description: New York, NY: Routledge, 2020. |
Series: Routledge focus on business and management |
Includes bibliographical references and index.
Identifiers: LCCN 2019018784 | ISBN 9780367142858 (hardback) |
ISBN 9780429031137 (ebook)
Subjects: LCSH: Liminality. | Psychology, Industrial. |
Organizational sociology.
Classification: LCC BF175.5.L55 T34 2020 | DDC 158.7—dc23
LC record available at https://lccn.loc.gov/2019018784

ISBN: 978-0-367-14285-8 (hbk)
ISBN: 978-0-429-03113-7 (ebk)

Typeset in Times New Roman
by codeMantra

To my father Ivo
        who loved books and taught me to love books

Contents

Preface

There is hardly a domain of science that has not been attracted by, and has not investigated, liminality, i.e., a stage of transition from a previous known state or role to a future one, over the past decades. From the original theorization offered by Victor Turner in anthropology on, the fascination for liminality has increasingly affected organization and management studies, but also medicine and health, sociology, tourism, and education research.

In organization studies, liminality can be traced back to heterogeneous situations that may prompt a suspension between states or roles: contingent workers who switch to different companies based on projects, consultants who operate at the boundaries between the consulting and the client companies, 'hybrid entrepreneurs' who start new ventures, while still keeping another job, or multiple careerists pursuing authenticity in more than one jobs simultaneously. Additionally, liminality is felt by managers who handle interorganizational relationships within customer-supplier networks, thus feeling at the edge of a set of heterogeneous organizations, or scientists who, albeit affiliated with R&D units, have strong ties with their scientific communities and acknowledge that they belong to neither settings thoroughly.

Liminality concerns also sociological processes like those related to migration flows (e.g., dwelling for a protracted time in an immigration center far away from home, longing for a future destination in which to settle down) and to detention (e.g., inmates and families who avail themselves of short stays in dedicated facilities, feeling neither at home nor in confinement). Liminality has been extensively delved into in medicine and in healthcare in general: for instance, cancer survivors are not sick anymore, but may perceive not to have totally recovered, and are stuck between life pre-cancer and life after cancer. On a related note, a perception of liminality affects disability when life can no longer be lived as it used to, and it is hard to envisage what lies ahead. From a yet different perspective, tourism has been interpreted as a realm of liminality, too: travels allow individuals to elude familiar settings and connections to disclose new views of self and experiment unforeseen courses of action.

Liminality is therefore a cross-disciplinary construct that enables us to shed light on heterogeneous social contexts which have been, however, explored in quite independent ways thus far. Although research focusing on this construct unanimously draws from Arnold van Gennep's and Victor Turner's seminal works, studies in different domains have tapped into specific features, such as the length of the liminal experience, the construction of individual practices to cope with the suspension that liminality engenders, the sense of belonging to a communitas among peers, or the reiteration of rites and ceremonies to accompany the transition. Consequently, only a partial outlook on liminality has been offered by recent contributions, especially in organization, impairing the understanding of the complex process that instead undergirds liminality.

This book proposes an elaboration of the liminal experience that integrates the stimuli offered by the various fields and represents a reference for more systemic further development on this topic. Chapter 1 analyzes the core elements of liminality based on the initial theorization provided by Victor Turner. In this perspective, liminality is essentially a phase of transition characterized by distinctive elements: rites, ceremonies, and symbols marking the separation from a previous state or role, the change under way, and the incorporation into the new one; the ambiguity of time flow and space that individuals in transition have to deal with and that have been labeled as timelessness and spacelessness; the disruption of a consolidated order, with its rules, hierarchies, and procedures, and the birth of an anti-structure; the development of egalitarian and empathetic ties with fellows undergoing a similar experience, which brings to the formation of communitas; and the identity work that individuals engage in to make sense of the loss of previous identities and identify possible selves to be realized in the future. In this perspective, rites, timelessness, spacelessness, anti-structure, communitas, and identity work altogether qualify liminality as a construct, while also underlining its difference from possibly close constructs like precariousness or identity conflict. The relevance of liminality can be grasped in light of its aftermath: on one hand, liminal experiences prompt feelings of stress and anxiety that can be hard to handle but, on the other, bear expectations of creative thinking that can enrich professional and personal life.

Chapter 2 delves into liminality in organization studies. The growing impetus provided to research on this topic can be traced back to the profound changes that have been touching on work processes. Situations of suspension between a 'before' and an 'after' have been identified when individuals operate at the boundaries across different organizations, when they perform contingent work, when they hold multiple roles within a single organization, and when they pursue plural careers in parallel. Liminality has been observed in specific settings, too, such as teams facing unexpected and upsetting events and in the launch of entrepreneurial initiatives. Learning takes center stage in organizational contexts: not only is the relationship between individual and organizational learning controversial, but the very benefits for workers in terms of development of competencies are called into question.

Chapter 3 widens the perspective on liminality to hints ensuing from a multiplicity of fields beyond the organizational domain able to inform our understanding of the core elements of the construct under study. Emergent views on liminality propose that liminality may be protracted, and not a short-lived process, and that it can be repeated over time in the personal and professional life. Additionally, liminality appears to be a dynamic process throughout which its basic features undergo a transformation, while multiple liminal experiences can be faced simultaneously. Latest contributions have also raised the issue that there might be various degrees of intensity of liminality within a given state or role based on individuals' liminality 'muscle' or competence grown out of former experiences. Finally, recent developments have also posed emphasis on individual, rather than collective, as advanced in Turner's studies, responses to the increasing deinstitutionalization of the contexts within which liminal experiences unfold.

In Chapter 4, the topics analyzed in the previous sections and that draw from reflection in fields that go beyond organization and anthropology are integrated into a revised interpretation of liminal experiences that paves the way for further qualitative research—which has represented the prevailing methodological approach so far in empirical studies on liminality—as well as for the much evoked quantitative research.

This book draws from a range of sources. A first selection was performed through a search on the Scopus database for articles that contained the words liminality, liminal, or liminar in the title, in the abstract, or as keywords, without any field filters. Subsequently, a snowball approach was adopted based on the citations contained in this set of papers. The collection was complemented by books that dealt with liminality applying similar criteria. Overall, 371 articles and 30 books were looked up.

Before starting the journey along the research on liminality with a focus on organization studies, I wish to express my gratefulness to Vando Borghi and Maria Alessandra Stefanelli: their constant support and valuable insightfulness have offered me precious motivation. I would like to thank also Giacomo Carli and Donato Cutolo for sharing the passion for liminality through lively and always stimulating discussions.

1 The Foundations of Liminality

Introduction

Approaching the fascinating topic of liminality cannot refrain from undertaking a journey that starts with its original, and maybe still more influential, theorization, which resides in anthropology, specifically in Arnold van Gennep's and Victor Turner's works. In those early contributions, all the relevant aspects of liminality were introduced and have inspired a growing body of studies in heterogeneous fields, ranging from sociology to organizational behavior, from medicine and health to education, and from tourism to marketing. In this chapter, the core features of the liminal experience are presented and discussed, taking move from the very interpretations provided by anthropological research, to then take into account subsequent elaborations and perspectives offered in other domains that have refined, enriched, and sometimes contrasted the initial framework. Beginning with a definition of liminality, the change of space and time rhythm that liminality entails, the role of rites, ceremonies, and symbols to signal the separation from a former situation, the unfolding of a liminal experience, and the incorporation into a new situation, the breakage of a consolidated and familiar order, the formation of strong ties among individuals sharing a similar experience, and the identity work that is related to the loss of previously held identities, the ambiguity of the current identities, and the possible elaboration of new ones for the future, will be delved into distinctive elements of liminality. Liminal processes can be fruitful and rewarding, but also unsettling and threatening: their positive outcomes as well as their 'dark side' need to be investigated to raise awareness about the likelihood of their coming together in most liminal experiences, which makes the overall picture complex and challenging.

Between and Betwixt: Experiencing Transitions

The concept of liminality can be almost unanimously traced back to the anthropological studies made by Arnold van Gennep at the beginning of the 20th century and subsequently revitalized and enriched by Victor Turner (1967, 1969, 1974a, b, 1975). The term 'liminality' stems from the Latin *Limen* or threshold, and refers to the central stage of transition from a previous, known situation to a new one that can be anticipated to varying degrees in different transitions (Figure 1.1). The starting point of a transition, which is the separation from a former state, is usually clearer than the endpoint, i.e., the incorporation into a new state: in other words, what is left behind is more familiar than what may lie ahead. In Turner's own words (1969, p. 80), liminality is 'a cultural realm that has few of the attributes of the previous or coming state' and in which the liminal subject, also called liminar, is a 'passenger.' In the anthropological domain, passages occur—and are unavoidable—as a consequence of changes in natural rhythms and human life. In small, rural societies, according to van Gennep (1960), liminality is experienced whenever a significant move is recorded, be it in the environment—for instance, the subsequence of seasons throughout the year—or in human existence, such as the transition from adolescence to adulthood or from singlehood to marriage. While van Gennep underlined the ordinary and almost peaceful pace of liminality, Turner (1974b), who later intensively built on van Gennep's reflection that was quite overlooked at the time, highlighted the likely strain that passages entail for individuals, imbuing liminality with a 'drama' connotation. Being originally entrenched in the ethnographic observation of tribes, and especially focusing on the Zambian Ndembu tribe members facing the transition from adolescence to adulthood, liminality emerges as both an individual experience, i.e., that of the single youngster facing the relinquishment of previous habits

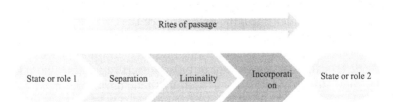

Figure 1.1 Stages of a transition. Adapted from van Gennep (1960) and Söderlund and Borg (2018).

and routines to embrace a new status and related responsibilities, and a collective experience that people in the same situation—for instance, all the tribe youngsters turning into adults—jointly handle (Turner, 1967). In his latest contributions on liminality, Turner (1974a) delved into the societal level that can be affected by liminality, making the example of cruel events like revolutions as well as of more playful moments like carnival celebrations.

Individuals who find themselves in between two different states or roles, one of which is a former familiar one, while the latter may still linger relatively obscure, are dominated by feelings of ambiguity and uncertainty that are meaningfully expressed by Turner (1969, p. 95):

> The attributes of liminality or liminal personae ('threshold people') are necessarily ambiguous, since this condition and these persons elude or slip through the networks of classifications that normally locate states and positions in cultural space. Liminal entities are neither here nor there; they are betwixt and between the positions assigned and arrayed by law, custom, conventions.
>
> (Turner, 1969, p. 95)

Based on this statement, liminars have since been identified in almost all the fields that have taken this construct into account as being 'betwixt and between', since they are 'temporarily undefined' (Turner, 1982, p. 27).

The perception of suspension is a major feature of liminal experiences that has been variously addressed in literature. Several meaningful metaphors have been evoked to account for the sense of indeterminateness proved by liminars, such as 'social limbo' (Cohn, 2001; Richter, 2016; Bamber, Allen-Collinson, and McCormack, 2017), 'black hole' associated with visions of 'drowning' and 'nightmare' (Kornberger, Justesen, and Mouritsen, 2011), 'gray area' and 'twilight zone' (Pina e Cunha, Guimarães-Costa, Rego, and Clegg, 2010; Hoel Felde, 2011), or a 'miasma of sociocultural categorizations and perceptions' (Cody and Lawlor, 2011, p. 216). The most pertinent way to express what being in the middle of a transition is like is to refer to it as a liminal experience according to the definition offered by Szakolczai (2009, p. 148): 'an "experience" means that once previous certainties are removed and one enters a delicate, uncertain, malleable state; something might happen to one that alters the very core of one's being.'

Transitional in-betweenness has peculiar features that make the experience of liminality unique, namely timeliness and spacelessness, rites and ceremonies, anti-structure, communitas, and identity work, which will be analyzed below.

Timeliness and Spacelessness

Liminality prompts deconstruction, confusion, and disorientation in time and space in those who cope with it, as Turner stated when talking about the specific 'units of space and time' inhabited by liminars:

> Units of space and time in which behaviour and symbolism are momentarily enfranchised from the norms and values that govern the public lives of incumbents of structural positions.
>
> (Turner, 1969, p. 166)

In the case of the Ndembu tribe studied by Turner, entering liminality implied that young people dwell in a detached place secluded from those who did not share their transition and in which they were deprived of opportunities to interact with the outside world (Turner, 1967). Turner (1974a, p. 58) stressed this connotation of liminality by stating that 'The passage from one social status to another is often accompanied by a parallel passage in space, a geographical movement from one place to another.'

Studies of liminality beyond anthropology have built on Turner's thought, underlining the perception of time and space as core aspects of a liminal experience (Cook-Sather, 2006; Wood, 2012; Winkler and Mahmood, 2015). Spaces can be not just dedicated locations that differ from those pertaining to non-liminars, as is the case with engineers working at a project in a separate location from colleagues who are not involved in the project (Wagner, Newell, and Kay, 2012), but also obscure and elusive places like hotels, where tourists stay for a few days while traveling and which are neither home nor an enduring destination (Pritchard and Morgan, 2006), or 'non-places' like call centers, shopping malls, and self-storages which can hardly nourish a sense of belonging and identification among employees and attendees (Daniel and Ellis-Chadwick, 2016; Karioris, 2016). Liminal space can be neutral (Tansley and Tietze, 2013), if not even become familiar over time, as commuters acknowledge for the trains or cars that daily take them back and forth from work (Wilhoit, 2017). Finally, liminal spaces can also turn out to be warm and friendly, as happens with the 'holding environment' that independent workers build to ease their precarious existence unfolding outside organizations (Petriglieri, Ashford, and Wrzesniewski, 2019) or that organizational members handling a severe crisis create to generate resilience (Powley, 2009; Teo, Lee, and Lim, 2017). Shortt (2015) provided convincing evidence of places that could be interpreted as liminal within the workplace precincts: stairwells, doorways, toilets, and storerooms were used by employees working in hair salons to escape the pressure they felt in the regular working areas, and were constructed as spaces in which to find some relief, develop a sense of belongingness, and cultivate creativity alongside co-workers. This finding is consistent with Dale and Burrell's (2008) consideration that some working zones may act as an alternative to dominant and clearly delineated areas in which to imagine and try out unconventional behaviors. Liminal space can be a welcoming context also if it is far away from the usual work environment, as is the case with a rural archipelago where individuals gather for a given period of time to elaborate and discuss new work practices or creative ideas (Vesala and Tuomivaara, 2018). Be they imbued with an ambiguous and potentially threatening meaning or, instead, with a neutral or even positive connotation, it is notable that liminal spaces elude ordinary work and life settings.

In a similar vein, the interpretation of time in liminality brings to the fore its undetermined nature. A significant gap between time experimented when dealing with transitions and in regular work or life circumstances emerges from reflection on this topic. Turner (1974a, p. 57) talked about the feeling of being '"out of time," that is, beyond or outside the time which measures secular processes and routines.' Delanty (2010, p. 31) enriched this interpretation resorting to the expression 'moments in and out of time' that individuals in transition from one state to another may live. Perception of undetermined time in liminality can last shortly, for instance, the duration of a consulting project, in line with the anthropological accounts provided by Turner, or, conversely, extend to longer periods, even epochs or eras (Thomassen, 2009).

Eluding the common flow, time passes either too fast or too slowly in liminal spaces, and work and life rhythms differ from how they used to be before embarking on the passage and from those perceived by people who do not face liminality (Vesala and Tuomivaara, 2018). Liminars recurrently speak of time and discuss how it passes by: in a study on universities as sites of transition between life at home and life as independent adults, first-year students evoke a so-called 'nostalgia for the present' (Karioris, 2016, p. 91). When they think about their future, they imagine locations, activities, and relationships that mirror their current situation; in parallel, the suspended time that they experience is translated into the future, as if the stage that they are undergoing could become a stable way of living. In this sense, 'time itself has moved in a polyrhythmic fashion. [...] Not only is time both fast and slow, but it is also empty and overflowing' (Karioris, 2016, p. 92).

The difference in time and space perception that liminars feel with respect to those who do not share their situation, alongside the ambiguity that these differences entail, has led to formulate the terms 'spacelessness' and 'timelessness' to depict the liminal condition (Kellerman, 2008; Küpers, 2011; Huang, Xiao, and Wang, 2018).

Rites, Ceremonies, and Symbols

Transitions are often solemnized by specific collective rites and ceremonies to signal the detachment from a previous, familiar situation and the succeeding incorporation into a new one (Cohn, 2001; Szakolczai, 2009; Kornberger et al., 2011). Turner (1982, p. 79) defined rituals as 'prescribed formal behavior for occasions not given over to technological routine, having reference to beliefs in invisible beings or powers regarded as the first and final causes of all effects.' Later contributions have underlined the very aim of rituals to communicate and underline the beginning and the end of passages:

> [Ritual is] a specific behavior or activity giving symbolic expression to feelings and thoughts. A ritual functions to mark a transition, to validate that an experience has occurred, to provide an occasion and location for confirming the reality of a new identity, and to stimulate the expression of memories and feelings associated with the transition.
>
> (Sleight, 2016, p. 55)

Van Gennep (1960) dealt in depth with rites denoting key life passages such as pregnancy, childbirth, and death in rural societies, and defined two types, respectively, anticipating and following the liminality experience: rites of separation and rites of incorporation. Rites of separation serve to celebrate the distance taken from old ways of acting and interacting to start a transition, whereas rites of incorporation have the objective to stress the endowment, at the end of the transition, with a new status or role.

At a higher level of abstraction, in his later contributions, Turner (1974a) identified rites characterizing the entry into a liminal condition as rites of effacement, aimed at signaling that customary routines, roles, and references must be dropped, and rites of ambiguity or paradox, which are bound to communicate the lack of clarity of the incoming liminal stage and its sharp difference from the former habitual state. Rites can be challenging, even humiliating, as is the case with the installation rite conferring the highest status *(Kanongesha)* to a senior chief in the Ndembu tribe described by Turner (1969), which implies nakedness of the people involved, insults, and images of death. Remarkably, rites are not plain demonstrations devoid of any practical content, but are meant to act as a guidance for action, as van Gennep (1960, p. 92) clearly stated: 'one should not forget that in the ceremonies of initiation in particular, the elders, instructors, or ceremonial chiefs recite what their other members of the group perform.' Turner (1982, p. 79) expanded on the essence of rites by writing that 'Rules "frame" the ritual process but the ritual process transcends its frame.' With reference to the *Kanongesha* rite, unpleasant aspects of initiation are a powerful reminder that chiefs nevertheless remain members of the community that they must dutifully and humbly serve.

Relevance of rites increases in highly institutionalized settings and decreases in less institutionalized ones (Söderlund and Borg, 2018). In general, rites tend to fade in contemporary societies in which a critic perspective prevails over a respectful abidance of rules and hierarchy (Boland, 2013; Adorno, 2015). In spite of this consideration, a wide range of less flamboyant rites and ceremonies are reported in modern organizational contexts to underscore liminal experiences. In consulting projects, which are commonly interpreted as liminal situations (Sturdy, Schwartz, and Spider, 2006; Sturdy, Handley, Clark, and Fincham, 2009), start-up meetings communicate investiture of consultants and divestiture of organizational members, whereas delivery and presentation of the final report can be likened to a ceremony of divestiture of consultants and (re)investiture of organizational members (Czarniawska and Mazza, 2003). In a related vein, divestiture and investiture rites accompany, respectively, the exit from the 'comfort zone' represented by one's own employing company and competencies, to enter an unfamiliar realm, and the later reincorporation into the familiar context with renewed competencies and revised professional and personal identities (Ryan, 2019).

Similarly, in the education field, involvement in 'stretch projects' (short-term projects aimed at developing students' autonomy), passing professional exams, and undertaking Master's qualifications have all been traced back to ceremonies signaling the transition to new, yet relatively undefined states (Tansley and Tietze, 2013).

In addition to rites, liminality can be characterized by specific symbols associated with the experience of passage (van Gennep, 1960; Turner, 1967). Symbols can be defined as 'things regarded by general consent as naturally typifying or representing, or recalling something by possession of analogous qualities or by association in fact or thought' (Turner, 1967, p. 19). In describing Ndembu rituals, Turner (1969, p. 360) referred to the 'rich proliferation of liminal symbols' and the 'symbolic milieu' that accompany initiations with a long period of seclusion similar to the induction into secret societies, and detailed how symbols act as a powerful means to indicate the dramatic change undergirding transitions (Turner, 1969, p. 359):

> Liminal entities, such as neophytes in initiation or puberty rites, may be represented as possessing nothing. They may be disguised as monsters, wear only a strip of clothing, or even go naked, to demonstrate that as liminal beings they have no status, property, insignia, secular clothing indicating rank or role, position in a kinship system - in short, nothing that may distinguish them from their fellow neophytes or initiands.

Dominant symbols, i.e., symbols that 'occupy the central role in ritual processes and are rather broad repositories for complex congeries of referents' (Wieting, 1972, p. 145), can have distinctive properties (Turner, 1967). They can represent more elements at the same time (condensation of meanings), they can collapse heterogeneous meanings (unification of meanings), or they can juxtapose the ideological pole, inspired by principles of social organization and moral values, and the sensory pole, made up of the natural and physical features (polarization of meanings).

In order for rituals to be productive for transitions, they must remain vital, though. A ritual's vitality resides in its ability to keep a coherent system of narratives and symbols that is meaningful to a given community (Campbell, 1972; Petriglieri and Petriglieri, 2010). If rituals become empty representations that do not convey sense anymore, then they are no longer apt to accompany individuals throughout their journey from a previous state or role to a subsequent one.

The Anti-Structure

Facing a transition requires that a familiar structure of rules, procedures, and roles, with its inner constraints, but also protection, be quit to be exposed to the novelty and the uncertainty of what may lie ahead (van Gennep, 1960). Individuals have to experiment with an anti-structure, as Turner has labeled the condition of living in an antithesis to the regular social order, during liminality. Anti-structure is, in one of the definitions provided by same author, the 'dissolution of normative social structure, with its role-sets, statuses, jural rights and duties, and so on' (Turner, 1974a, p. 60). The anti-structure implies that individuals be deprived of their established points of reference, and left vulnerable and 'naked; unranked of anything that differentiates them from others—they are temporarily fallen through the cracks; in the interstices of social structure where they are most aware of themselves' (Adorno, 2015, p. 103). Anti-structure stands in marked contrast with the structure to which those who are not liminal still comply with, but may serve, over time, as an inspiration to change the structure itself (Bigger, 2009; Szakolczai, 2009; Atkinson and Robson, 2012; Hodgson and Paton, 2016; Daniel and Ellis-Chadwick, 2016; Bamber et al., 2017). When liminality has been examined at a societal level, for instance, revolutions have been likened to transitions that can shape the new arising society by replacing the well-set structure with the anti-structure that rebels have created while preparing for the fight (Thomassen, 2012). Remarkably, as Thomassen (2009, p. 23) affirmed, 'While liminality is "unstructure", a lack of fixed points in a given moment, it must at the same time be considered the origin of structure.'

Being freed from structural order and tackling an anti-structure does not entail a void of roles and routines, in fact. The breakage of a consolidated order prompts a 'play of *meanings*, involving the reversal of hierarchical orderings of values and social statuses' (Turner, 1981, p. 62, italics in the original) to be gradually filled with emergent rules. New rules may even imbue a potentially free domain with conventional wisdom, thus reducing the likely dramatic effect of transitioning (Cook-Sather, 2006). Anti-structure is therefore ambivalent: it can represent an alternative and subvert taken-for-granted order, but also become a source of rigidity and inertia over time.

The anti-structure has been also populated with formal roles from early anthropological studies on. Neophytes undertaking passages in tribes were in fact supervised by seasoned and respected members of their group—usually the elders—who drove them throughout the passage, setting the rules to be observed, the tasks to be performed, and the rhythms to be followed (Turner, 1969, 1974b). These formal roles usually serve a positive function, in that they act as guideposts for disoriented and doubtful people (Thomassen, 2015): in anthropology, they were designated as 'masters of ceremonies' or 'absolute rulers' to point to their relevance in designing and managing the anti-structure (Turner, 1967, pp. 99–100). As in any power games, positive roles have their counterpart: 'tricksters' try to subvert and rule out any beneficial influence exerted by masters and rulers, mocking the newly established order as well as its supporters (Turner, 1967; Szakolczai, 2009). Tricksters are familiar with liminality and tend to dwell in that situation, in which they thrive and which they have no intention to quit (Söderlund and Borg, 2018). Relationships between positive and negative influencers are often conflicting, sometimes even in a stormy way: if masters and rulers give up on contrasting tricksters and abdicate their function to indicate the pathway to be followed, tricksters may end up prevailing and becoming charismatic leaders for liminars (Pace and Pallister-Wilkins, 2018).

Communitas

Strong ties usually develop among individuals sharing a liminal experience, leading to the formation of a communitas. Once again, Turner's original words convey the essence of what a community is about. The author tapped into the need for connection that people handling a similar transition might feel, talking about the aspiration to 'human interrelatedness' (1974a, p. 74) and the 'nature of "interstructural" human beings' (1967, p. 93). The search for social support from peers coming to terms with a common passage is rooted, in Turner's work (1982, p. 47), in the placing of a 'high value on personal honesty, openness, and lack of pretensions' that the 'neither here nor there' fosters. Individuals feel the imperative to establish links to overcome the uncertainty that liminality engenders: in social settings like the tribes investigated by anthropologists, through a heightened sense of togetherness, liminality transcends an individual occurrence and becomes a common experience (Turner, 1969).

Bonds unfolding among liminars are 'undifferentiated, equalitarian, extant, nonrational, existential' (Turner, 1974b, p. 174) and based upon empathy and solidarity. The unprompted nature of these ties has led to the introduction of the concept of communitas as 'an unstructured or rudimentarily structured and relatively undifferentiated *comitatus*, community, or even communion of equal individuals who submit together to the general authority of the ritual elders' (Turner, 1969, p. 96). The communitas is therefore the informal getting together of individuals who address a common transition and look for comfort and encouragement from each other. Turner (1974a) theorized about different types of communitas: a spontaneous community underlies 'a direct, immediate and total confrontation of human identities' that eludes 'role, status, reputation, class, caste, sex, or other structural niche' (p. 79). An ideological communitas represents the effort to conceptualize, through the use of language and cultural artifacts, the values, beliefs, and patterns of behavior characterizing a spontaneous grouping of individuals. Finally, the social constraints linking peers who face a same liminal condition can become so strong that the 'the *experience* of communitas becomes the *memory* of communitas' (Turner, 1974a, p.78, italics in the original). Normative communitas legitimize and thus institutionalize the relationships and concepts undergirding spontaneous and normative communitas: they spawn a 'perduring social system' in which affective bonds between specific individuals turn into depersonalized ties among 'social personae' (Turner, 1974a, p. 78). Under these circumstances, a normative communitas merges with and integrates the anti-structure, thereby enriching the initial endowment of recreated roles, rites, and symbols with a more articulated set of rules, routines, and interactions arising from voluntary ties.

Literature has offered various examples of the comradeship that can accompany liminars throughout their transition (Huang et al., 2018; O'Loughlin et al., 2017). An intersubjective agreement based upon an egalitarian stance has been shown to increase individuals' resilience in the wake of unexpected and threatening events (Powley, 2009; Pina e Cunha et al., 2010). Powley (2009) tapped into the way members of a school that had gone through a major disruption caused by a standoff and shooting found solace, and increased their resilience to overcome the perception of being suspended between an old, reassuring world and an uncertain future, in the social connections that they established after the accident.

A sense of deeply bonding with individuals dwelling in a 'gray area' was reported also in medical settings (Murphy, 1987; Murphy, Scheer, Murphy, and Mack, 1988). Parents of children with special needs set linkages to confront their respective situations and shared ways of coping when sitting in the waiting room while their children were undertaking treatment (Cohn, 2001). Likewise, solidarity among cancer patients who have ended active cure and feel to be between two worlds—that of health and that of sickness, or that of life and death—allows them to embark upon a common spiritual journey that sparks growth and transcendence (Adorno, 2015). In general, communitas flourish in the form of support groups among people sharing a similar disease, since these latter act as allies and sources of relief for each other in handling the liminal experience (Brown, Huszar, and Chapman, 2017).

Organizational studies have been paying increasing attention to the relationships among liminars lately. Among the different tactics that unemployed resorted to during the so-called Greek depression triggered by the 2008 Global Financial Crisis, besides trying to retrieve their previous jobs or carving out future job alternatives, they coalesced with each other to create arrangements in which to collectively engage in original work processes and generate new products and services (Daskalaki and Simosi, 2018). These joint spaces can be likened to anti-structures challenging the existing order and proposing unconventional ways of organizing. Communitas can also develop during a project performance, which, as will be discussed in Chapter 3, is deemed as a liminal situation, when an egalitarian outlook towards team members can rule out established rank and status difference (Wagner et al., 2012). A form of kinship can also stem from creative professionals' sharing of a liminal experience on a secluded island with the aim to elaborate on new work practices (Vesala and Tuomivaara, 2018).

There may be a dark side to communitas, though. Power games can develop over time within a communitas and transform the personal and open relationships that give bith to it: in these cases, a hierarchical ordering arises that makes the liminal experience resemble the regular structure operating outside (Atkinson and Robson, 2012). In the case of patients struggling against potentially chronicle diseases like myalgic encephalomyelitis and chronic fatigue syndrome, sufferers, who fall between 'socially recognised and medically sanctioned categories' (Brown et al., 2017, p. 696) and therefore are deemed to be liminal, build strong links that help them share their stories and search for advice from each other. Those who finally recover, however, cope with an unpleasant refusal to accept their betterment from communitas members who are still struggling and tie them to their previous identity and condition as sick people. Consequently, recovered individuals have to handle a new form of liminality, as they no longer feel to belong to the unhealthy people's domain, nor are they fully integrated into the healthy people's world. It has been even conjectured that communitas become replete with negative feelings among peers such as resentment, suspect, and animosity, if liminality conditions are hard to withstand and competition, instead of cooperation, enables survival and thriving (Thomassen, 2009).

Identity Work

Undertaking transitions prompts questioning who one currently is and who might become, while letting go of previously held assumptions and beliefs about who one was (Szakolczai; 2009; Ladge, Clair, and Greenberg, 2012; Hodgson and Paton, 2016; Söderlund and Borg, 2018). A focus on identity, which can be positioned within the concept of identity work, i.e., the set of activities aimed at 'forming, repairing, maintaining, strengthening or revising [identity] constructions that are productive of a sense of coherence and distinctiveness' (Sveningsson and Alvesson, 2003, p. 1165), has accompanied the reflection on liminality since its early beginning (van Gennep, 1960; Turner, 1974a, 1977). Identity work is in fact particularly intense and necessary when individuals are neither one thing nor the other, and a disruption of the sense of self occurs (Beech, 2008, 2011). According to Beech (2011), liminars can embark upon one or more practices to elaborate on the future self that differ in terms of the dialogical interplay between the individual (inside) and the others (outside):

> Liminality in identity work can be constituted by one or more of these practices: experimentation, in which the liminar constructs and projects an identity; reflection, in which the liminar considers the views of others and questions the self; and recognition, in which the liminar reacts to an identity that is projected onto them.
>
> (p. 291)

While experimentation represents an inside-out orientation and recognition expresses a reaction to others' projections, it is only reflection that spurs a two-way intertwining between the individual and the social context in which he or she is nested.

As seen above, a very function of rites and ceremonies is the formalization of the detachment from a traditional way of being to embark on a pathway towards a definition of self that is still fairly unknown

(Kornberger et al., 2011). Embracing liminality requires that individuals first cope with a process of identity loss, in which long-held central and distinctive attributes of the self are left behind (Conroy and O'Leary-Kelly, 2014; Söderlund and Borg, 2018). A process of transformation of the self therefore is coupled with, and underlies, liminality (Atkinson and Robson, 2012; Hoyer and Steyaert, 2015). This process is dynamic and does not necessarily end up with a clear, unambiguous redefinition of self according to post-Turner interpretations of liminality: the longer liminality lasts, the more fluctuating identity may become, without a specific 'endpoint' (Ybema, Beech, and Ellis, 2011). As Ellis and Ybema (2010, p. 299) claim, managers in charge of handling interorganizational relationships on a long-term basis develop an interpretation of themselves as continuously 'oscillating between "in" and "out," "same" and "other," and between an inclusive and exclusive "us," with no new sharp identity emerging as time flows. In these accounts, the liminar nurtures a mutable view of self and does not tend towards a definite self-representation, as the liminal experience unfolds. Liminality can thus be linked to the wavering across 'conflicting loyalties and obligations' (Zabusky and Barley, 1997; Ybema et al., 2011, p. 25).

There can be another outcome of identity work in protracted liminality, however, i.e., the elaboration and negotiation of a new identity that may get validated over time. This evolution applies to Murphy's sensemaking of his quadriplegia developed from a spinal tumor (Murphy, 1987; Murphy et al., 1988; Murphy, 1995). All the previously examined aspects can be found in his experience: the transition from healthy person to a person with special needs, the change of space and time (e.g., hospitals and treatment cycles) that characterizes getting accustomed to the novel state, the rites that signal the entrance into an uncertain and destabilizing condition, and the struggle to realize who the person is and who may become. The identity work performed alongside healthcare professionals, family, and other patients that stems from lingering in the 'gray area' that sickness stands for can lead to the interiorization of a new self-representation as a person with a disability which paves the way for (re)incorporation into a collective (Reid-Cunningham, 2009).

A major feature of identity work in liminal experiences lies in the very opportunity to identify and try on possible selves that were not accessible before the transition (Atkinson and Robson, 2012; Hoyer and Steyaert, 2015). A possible self refers to who a person might become in the future, in the work and/or in the private life sphere (Markus and Nurius, 1986; Ibarra, 2004; Obodaru, 2012). Due to the loss of previous points of reference and the exposure to different space, time rhythm, patterns of interaction, and emergent sets of routines, liminality offers the chance to experiment with new view of self to tend to. Liminality in fact provides stimuli for a 're-authoring of self' or 'undoing the script' (Land, Rattray, and Vivian, 2014, p. 201) in which individuals try out, question, adopt, or reject new identities and related ways of acting (Hawkins and Edwards, 2015; Garcia-Lorenzo, Donnelly, and Sell-Trujillo, 2018). A meaningful example is conveyed by Ladge et al. (2012) when parsing out pregnancy as a liminal experience: while getting ready for childbirth, women carve out images of what kind of mothers they can become, how their professional identity might change, and how the modification of their personal and professional identities might be interwoven.

Liminality as a sort of 'playground' for experimenting with identities that could not be imagined within consolidated perspectives led Ibarra and Obodaru (2016) to propose an 'identity play' concept, with the aim to underline the potential to engage in the trial of possible selves that liminality entails. Individuals coping with liminality in fact should first and foremost aspire 'to explore possible selves rather than to claim and be granted, desired, optimal or ought selves.' (Ibarra and Obodaru, 2016, p. 11), whereas identity work more generally concerns adaptation and modification of an extant identity or the adjustment to a new role's expectations (Snow and Anderson, 1987; Ibarra and Barbulescu, 2010; Brown, 2015). Identity play enables the exploration of an array of identity options, while delaying closure and commitment to a specific one (Ibarra and Petriglieri, 2010): liminars can then be seen as enjoying the valuable chance of undertaking more identity work than individuals in regular situations.

Liminality as a Realm of Possibilities, but also a Domain of Anguish

Transitioning across states or roles is not devoid of contradictions: while it can open up a range of opportunities that could not be previously envisioned, as argued above, it can also convey threats and spark fears. Experiencing liminality is therefore a complex process that may be filled with a sense of growth and fulfilment as well as with feelings of loss and vulnerability. In the subsequent paragraphs, the most relevant outcomes of liminality that extant studies have brought up so far will be analyzed.

The Creative Power of Liminal Personae

Taking distance from a formerly known situation without being fully aware of what lies ahead offers the often-unparalleled chance to explore a range of possible roads to take. In fact, 'in liminality people "play" with the elements of the familiar and defamiliarize them. Novelty emerges from unprecedented combinations of familiar elements' (Turner, 1974a, p. 60). Going beyond the initial puzzlement that ensues from the loss of taken-for-granted points of reference, the release from usual constraints provides 'a fructile chaos, storehouse of possibilities' (Turner, Bruner, and Geertz, 1986, p. 42). Turner recurrently underlined the potential of liminality to spawn change, stating that 'In this gap between ordered worlds almost anything may happen' (1974b, p. 13) and that a liminal space is 'a realm of pure possibility whence novel configurations of ideas and relations may arise' (1967, p. 97).

Creativity ensues from the very disruption of the regular structure and involvement in an anti-structure that pertain to liminality. Exposure to the breakage of the consolidated order becomes a forum for exploration (Cook-Sathers, 2006; Bigger, 2009). Individuals take advantage of the freedom that they enjoy compared to the previous constraints to which they were subjected—and by which others still have to abide—to experiment with playfulness and envisage new courses of action (Pritchard and Morgan, 2006; Howard-Grenville, Golden-Biddle, Irwin, and Mao, 2011; Cronin, Ryrie, Huntley, and Hayton, 2018). Along this line of reasoning, liminality can be regarded as 'fruitful darkness' (Cody and Lawlor, 2011, p. 223) that brings to the fore unimagined pathways to be investigated and exploited. This opportunity appears to affect also the most unpleasant liminal experiences, such as late-stage cancer patients who, in spite of their critical condition, can undergo a process of growth and transcendence, sustained by healthcare professionals and relatives, identifying new meaning in their sufferance (Adorno, 2015).

Promising avenues for creativity have been highlighted especially in organizational studies. In general, liminality represents a valuable chance for organizations to revise their consolidated rules and routines, thereby lessening rigidities and resistance to change (Küpers, 2011). Sankowska and Söderlund (2015) stressed the potential for positive transformations both at an individual and at a collective level that liminality related to mobile work can entail, such as modifying and integrating knowledge structures already detained and eliciting social reflexivity on work practices. On a related note, Hoyer and Steyaert (2015) stressed how liminality stemming from career changes can be confusing and emotionally challenging, since it points to the co-existence of coherence and ambiguity, but also foster a healing process through the possibility to elaborate on a desired work future. A particularly favorable setting is represented by entrepreneurial initiatives: in these cases, which can involve the resort to self-storage spaces (Daniel and Ellis-Chadwick, 2016), a 'structural meltdown' paves the way for envisioning and testing new organizational forms (Garcia-Lorenzo et al., 2018, p. 378). Entrepreneurship is here seen as a transitional and transformative situation for underemployed people in which possible future states and selves are first imagined and then tentatively brought into being: liminality becomes therefore the opportunity to 'rebuild self, projects and social relationships' (Garcia-Lorenzo et al., 2018, p. 381). Nascent entrepreneurs who are appraising prospective courses of action and therefore feel detached from their traditional occupations intertwine changes in the entrepreneurial self and changes in their holding environment through creative exchanges with different actors. Liminality thus not only inspires critical thinking but also urges improvisation and invention. Similarly, Greek unemployed workers availed themselves of their liminal position in society to design and implement alternative organizational forms, such as the joint refurbishment of dismissed factories, that in the end were able to challenge the dominant economic order (Daskalaki and Simosi, 2018). The creative power prompted by liminality therefore can go beyond its starting point—a set of would-be entrepreneurs in the case under study—to likely impact upon a wider collective. This larger-scale effect had been conjectured by Turner when talking about the relationship between cultural creativity and freewheeling in liminality and its potential for societal change: from liminal situations, innovation is brought to 'the "central" economic and politico-legal domains and arenas' (Turner, 1974a, p. 60). Even when creativity is taken into account, the likelihood of liminality to affect a larger community was underscored by Turner, thus increasing the relevance of this construct.

The Negative Feelings Associated with Liminality

Besides the expectations of freedom and creativity that liminality bears, there are also drawbacks in being 'between and betwixt.' Turner (1969, p. 95) likened liminality to feelings of 'wilderness' and 'invincibility,' but also to fears of 'death' and 'darkness.' The contemporary existence of positive and negative attitudes towards liminality has resonated with most reflection on this construct. The loss of familiar points of reference and previous routines and patterns of interactions that transitions entail paves the way for the ambivalence of this experience. According to Küpers (2011, p. 51), liminality can be both 'exhilarating and frustrating.' Quitting familiar habits, while uncertainty about the future is looming, can in fact imbue individuals with stress, anxiety, and the perception of a poignant lack of affiliation. Being contingent workers switching to different projects and different organizations, for example, lets individuals unsure about what may be waiting for them in terms not only of forthcoming appointments, but also of real work opportunities (Garsten, 1999). Under the same circumstances, individuals can feel to have less power than the regular workers with whom they collaborate in the client firms, thus ending up with a sense of frustration (Tempest and Starkey, 2004). Interacting with temporary work agencies to be assigned to client companies to carry out projects, as well as being scientists in R&D units while also active members of scientific communities, pose a challenge to professionals in terms of competing loyalties, underlining their lack of belongingness (Zabusky and Barley, 1997; Iedema, Degeling, Braithwaite, and White, 2004; Borg and Söderlund, 2013). As Zabuski and Barley (1997) stressed, scientists at the crossroads of firms and scientific communities may experience puzzlement, since they fully belong neither here nor there. The negative feelings ensuing from liminality may be so cumbersome to resemble 'monsters of doubt' (Hawkins and Edwards, 2015, p. 24; Daniel and Ellis-Chadwick, 2016, p. 7) that rule out any benefits of a passage. In some contexts, when liminality ceases being a stage of transition to become a 'trap' from which it is difficult to get out, as happens with teaching-only positions in British universities whose incumbents know that they will hardly or never turn to more appealing research positions, no creativity is likely to emerge, while anxiety and dissatisfaction prevail (Bamber et al., 2017). The social consequences of liminality can be burdensome, too: the development of information system projects can be regarded as liminal experiences owing to the creation of a dedicated workspace (Wagner et al., 2012). The same environment built ad hoc to sustain the project activities, though, freeing team members from habitual routines and reducing interference from the outside, can lead to a growing sense of marginalization. Isolated in their location and bound to interact mainly with each other, team members in fact feel cut out of organizational life, with its constraints, but also with its continuous stimuli and dynamism.

Finally, most studies on the aftermath of liminality point to their ambivalence and do not focus on positive or negative outcomes only. Performing contingent work allows for valuable opportunities for creativity and self-experimentation, but it can also be interpreted as an endangering situation bringing about precariousness and fear (Tempest and Starkey, 2004). A similar consideration applies to liminality in tourism: staying at a hotel is deemed as a liminal experience that mingles features of openness, such as the possibility to enact transgressive behaviors usually inhibited in familiar locations, and of oppression, such as being under the control of video surveillance systems (Pritchard and Morgan, 2006).

The Liminoid Experience

In his later writings, Turner advanced also the likelihood of liminoid experiences. 'Liminoid' refers to voluntary experiences of detachment from usual ways of living and social constraints that are individually chosen, rather than socially expected or imposed, and mostly develop in a short-term span. The voluntary and individual nature differentiates liminoid from liminal experiences: as Turner (1974a, p. 74) stated, 'Optation pervades the liminoid phenomenon, obligation the liminal. One is all play and choice, an entertainment, the other is a matter of deep seriousness, even dread, it is demanding, compulsory.' Even more clearly, Turner (1974a, p. 86) argued that '[The liminoid] is often *commodity*, which one pays and selects for [...] One *works at* the liminal, one *plays with* the liminoid' (italics in the original), to underline playful and lightweight content of the liminoid.

Liminoid experiences were associated by Turner with leisure genres such as drama, literature, and sports, which individuals can pursue freely and as long as they wish, without any formal obligations. Albeit predominantly an individual effort, the liminoid can have a mass or collective effect when the new ideas and practices generated in these situations pervade society, introducing innovation. If liminality has been originally conceived of in tribal and early agrarian communities, the liminoid phenomenon applies to complex, post-industrial societies in which individuals enjoy greater margins of autonomy and the availability of a larger variety of resources. Although liminoid experiences are still scarcely investigated and rely mainly on Turner's elaboration, it is noteworthy that, in his thought, universities and research institutes tend to be liminoid contexts in which freewheeling likely happens: the ideas that are produced in these settings convey innovation to society at large (Turner, 1974a). Consequently, liminoid phenomena, as well as liminal phenomena, act as laboratories for creativity that have the potential to challenge the consolidated order. A notable exception to the scarce attention devoted to the liminoid is the study by Vesala and Tuomivaara (2018) on 32 creative professionals, e.g., journalists, graphic designers, and advertisement consultants, who spontaneously decided to spend a week working together in small groups on a secluded island where they were detached from any external connections as well as from familiar roles and routines. During this liminoid experience, as the authors labeled it, in which work and life rhythms had substantially changed and a sense of communitas grew as a consequence of sharing the same space, peers could elaborate, discuss, and refine new work practices to be later brought into their jobs. Original ideas originated from participants' decision to take a distance from well-established space and time to throw themselves, albeit on a temporary basis, into an alien physical and social environment.

Conclusion

Approaching liminality cannot refrain from delving into its roots in anthropology, in particular first in van Arnold Gennep's and then in Victor Turner's contributions. Based on their writings and subsequent further elaborations in various fields, the core aspects of a liminal experience, intended as a stage of the transition between a former well-known situation to a looming, often uncertain one, can be delineated (Table 1.1). Dealing with liminality implies that the space inhabited and the work and lifetime rhythm change, that an anti-structure replaces the social structure of the 'outside' world, articulating alternative roles, procedures, and norms, and that strong ties develop among individuals going through the same experience. In the original interpretation of liminality, rites, ceremonies, and symbols specifically designed accompany liminars along the process signaling its beginning, marking its happening,

Table 1.1 The core elements of a liminal experience

Core elements	Main content	Main references
Timelessness and spacelessness	Experiencing different units of time and space from incumbents of established positions	Turner (1969); Cook-Sather, (2006); Wood (2012); Tansley and Tietze (2013); Winkler and Mahmood (2015)
Rites, ceremonies, and symbols	Collective practices marking the beginning, the unfolding, and the end of transitions	Van Gennep (1960); Szakolczai (2009); Kornberger et al. (2011); Sleight (2016)
Anti-structure	Disrupting consolidated order and laying the premises for an alternative one	Turner, 1974a; Bigger, 2009; Szakolczai, 2009; Thomassen (2009); Atkinson and Robson, 2012; Bamber et al. (2017)
Communitas	Building egalitarian and empathetic relationships among liminars	Turner (1969, 1977); Murphy (1987); Murphy et al. (1988); Cohn (2001); Adorno (2015)
Identity work	Making sense of the loss of previous identities and imagining possible selves	van Gennep (1960); Turner (1974a, 1977); Beech (2011); Hawkins and Edwards (2015); Ibarra and Obodaru (2016); Garcia-Lorenzo et al. (2018)

and celebrating its end. Facing a transition is bound to prompt a deep-rooted questioning of who the person is while facing the passage, but also, and maybe above all, who he or she might become in the future.

The increasing interest for liminality that has been touching on a variety of fields over the past decades can be traced back not only to the possibility to interpret human behavior through this lens, but also to the complexity of the outcomes—both promising and threatening—that the reflection on this topic has stressed. Major breakthroughs in society can be introduced by the processes unfolding in liminal or liminoid situations: creativity and innovativeness are therefore expectations inextricably intertwined with the experience of a 'gray area.' At the same time, though, the uncertainty characterizing liminality may provoke anxiety and stress. In most situations, both positive and negative reactions are related to liminal experiences, so that rarely can polarized consequences—be they beneficial or potentially harmful—be expected.

Turner's theorization of liminality already comprised many of the aspects that have been brought to the fore in later research and that will be analyzed in the following chapters. To this regard, he was a forward-looking scholar, anticipating issues that have become relevant over time. The most striking, and perhaps not enough acknowledged in the literature, regards the duration of a liminal experience. Although fundamentally framed as a transient situation in the anthropological domain, Turner opened up the possibility that some liminal experiences may be long-lasting, if not even permanent. He introduced the idea of liminality turning into a 'tunnel' from which it is hard to escape: 'one finds in liminality both positive and active qualities, especially where that "threshold" is protracted and becomes a "tunnel," when the "liminal" becomes the "cunicular"' (Turner, 1974a, p. 72). What was initially conceived of as a well-defined transition, as shown in rural societies, may end up becoming a stable situation with no endpoint in sight. Turner seemed to suggest that permanent liminality be a source of discomfort and unease: this interpretation is partly put into question by the latest development on this issue, as will be discussed in Chapter 3.

Turner raised also awareness about the potential for increasing the benefits of liminality that technological progress could convey. He detected in fact a virtuous relationship between technology development and growing division of labor, which pertain to post-industrial organization of work, on one hand, and the enhanced 'experimentation with variable repertories' of liminal forms (1974a p. 83, cited from Sutton-Smith, 1972, p. 18), on the other. The introduction of the liminoid corresponded to the need to account for the different types of liminality expected in contemporary societies in comparison with the rural contexts in which it had been observed and theorized. Societal change and technological development, in other words, have paved the way for the diffusion of liminality in heterogenous domains, ranging from organization and management to sociology, and from medicine to education. In the formulation of liminality originated in anthropology, the features of liminality that have been delved into in this chapter, namely timelessness, spacelessness, anti-structure, rites, ceremonies and symbols, communitas, and identity work, were all contemporarily present. An experience, based on its original elaboration, relied on—and required—all of these aspects to be labeled as liminal. Thanks to this strong characterization, liminal and liminoid phenomena are interpretive lens to comprehend certain appealing spheres of human action, but not any situations of precariousness or uncertainty that individuals might encounter during the course of their life.

2 Liminality and Organizations

Introduction

Liminality has become an increasingly salient topic in the organizational debate lately. Most of the recognition that it has been receiving in this field is due to profound changes in work processes that have undermined some long-held perspectives. Work processes have in fact gradually marginalized a view of employment as relatively stable and implying the commitment to a limited number of organizations during the working life. Work has been tending towards contingency or short-term engagement, be it on a voluntary basis or induced by necessity. Additionally, it often unfolds across different organizations and may require the performance of different roles within a single organization or even the parallel assumption of different roles in different organizations. Within this fluidity of work arrangements, the likelihood to feel 'betwixt and between,' 'neither here nor there,' or 'both here and there,' in any case in transition and inhabiting a 'gray area,' is bound to intensify. Liminality has therefore become an interpretive lens to grasp the contemporary work scenario that appeals to organization scholars. This chapter will delve into liminality in the organizational field moving from changes in work processes to identify four main avenues of investigation: liminality across organizational borders, liminality as contingent work, liminality within an organization, liminality as the pursuit of plural careers.

In addition to these streams of research linked to work processes, this chapter will also analyze the attention that liminality has garnered in specific organizational settings, such as entrepreneurship and teams. Individuals who run a new venture while keeping another job (hybrid entrepreneurs) or who are trying to launch a new business idea (nascent entrepreneurs) have been considered as liminars, in that they are in between two different work domains or on the way to become just entrepreneurs, but not yet fully so. Liminality has been also traced back to teams, in particular to those that face unexpected and demanding adversities requiring them to exit their comfort zone and tackle uncertainty about the future. A notable characteristic of liminality in teams is the relevance of leadership, which is interconnected with the guidance needed to cope with, and survive, in extreme situations.

At a higher level, the intensity of resort to the forms of liminality that have been recalled above has the potential to affect organizations, not only individuals and groups, with the formation of a liminal organization that coexists and interacts with the regular structure.

In the organizational perspective, the outcomes of liminality take on a peculiar nuance. Learning processes take center stage: they are intertwined with identity work, with different and still controversial effects for the individuals and the organizations involved. Overall, the progress of research on liminality in the organizational field has borne on the core features of this experience that have been the object of Chapter 1: rites, ceremonies, and symbols; spacelessness and timelessness; anti-structure; communitas; identity work, which will be revised in the conclusive paragraph. Concerning these founding elements of liminality, it is remarkable that the egalitarian and supportive ties that link individuals sharing a similar experience are brought to the back in organizational speculation, while individual agency manifested through a range of tactics comes to the fore.

The Changing Nature of Work Arrangements and the Diffusion of Liminality

The recent flourishing of organizational studies on liminality is intertwined with the changing nature of work processes in the past decades. Boundaries across organizations and occupations have become growingly blurred, and a sense of uncertainty and a lack of stability have spread among workers (Barley and Kunda, 2001, 2004). Contemporary working life is characterized by frequent changes of jobs and organizations, so that individuals who remain committed to one and the same company are now almost memories of the past (Arthur, 2008; Petriglieri, Petriglieri, and Wood, 2018). Work is getting flexible and temporary (Arthur, Khapova, and Wilderom, 2005; Barley, Bechky, and Milliken, 2017): consequently, individuals can easily face transitions from one job to another, thus living liminal experiences recurrently in their life.

Contingent work has been on the rise both in practice and in academic reflection (Barley and Kunda, 2004; Connelly and Gallagher, 2004; Bidwell, Briscoe, Fernandez-Mateo, and Sterling, 2013; Katz and Krueger, 2016; Fisher and Connely, 2017). It can be defined as:

> Jobs that involve nonstandard employer-employee contracts where a standard contract is assumed to be a full-time, permanent employment relationship. Contingent work typically includes part-time work, work performed by independent contractors and on-call workers, and work done by temporary workers, hired either directly for limited-duration projects or through temporary help firm.
>
> (Blank, 1998, p. 258)

Workers can resort to contingent employment for a variety of often concurrent reasons (Kunda, Barley, and Evans, 2002; Barley and Kunda, 2004; Connelly and Gallagher, 2004; Caza, Moss, and Vough, 2017): they can react against the loss of a previous job by putting decisions on future employing companies on hold; they can opt for more remunerative contracts as freelancers; they can search for learning opportunities by switching work contexts and changing relationships; they can pursue authenticity in their sense of self through experimentation with different settings and the enjoyment of greater autonomy, or they even cannot have any other options in sight. Employing organizations have therefore in many cases ceased being a holding environment, i.e., 'a social context that reduces disturbing affect and facilitates sense making' (Petriglieri and Petriglieri, 2010, p. 50), in which individuals can engage in identity work to explore and test possible selves.

The new economic model called 'gig economy' has reinforced and given impetus to this trend. Taken from the music domain, the term 'gig' has started being used after the 2008 global financial crisis to refer to the small works—the 'gigs'—that individuals had to carry out due to the difficulty of finding stable and rewarding jobs. Sometimes, different works follow each other on a short-term basis, while in other cases, workers perform more jobs in parallel (Caza et al., 2017). Some data meaningfully testify to the changing landscape of employment in this direction. Full-time jobs are no longer the standard point of reference in Western societies, and the decoupling of job and work has been called into question, according to which individuals may not hold a job in terms of long-lasting appointment with a single organization, but carry out different works for different organizations (World Economic Forum, 2016; Work Employment Confederation, 2016). More than one-fifth of US jobs are no longer full time and permanent, and rates are also higher in other countries (McKinsey, 2016; Petriglieri, Ashford, and Wrzesniewski, 2019). Recent surveys reported that 'all of the net employment growth in the U.S. economy from 2005 to 2015 appears to have occurred in alternative work arrangements' (Katz and Krueger, 2016, p. 7).

In other words, individuals may be jobless, but not workless in the current economic scenario. In the United States, one-third of workers do not anymore have a regular eight-hour work, while the number of people working part-time has been steadily increasing (Galagan, 2013; Yellen, 2014; Valletta and van der List, 2015). Although an exhaustive and accurate appraisal of the diffusion of contingent work depends on what types of work can be properly included, its relevance is undeniable and bound to intensify (De Stefano, 2015; Katz and Krueger, 2016; Maniya et al., 2016; Hall and Krueger, 2018). Contingent work can differ in terms of workers' competencies: it can require basic skills, as is the case with food couriers, Uber drivers, and home services providers, but also advanced skills, as with crowdwork like Crowdsource and Clickworker (Pedulla, 2013; De Stefano, 2016). In engineering-intensive industries especially, work has been undergoing a 'projectification' and 'flexibilization' trend all over the world (Whittington, Pettigrew, Peck, Fenton, and Conyon, 1999; Kalleberg, 2001, 2003; Söderlund, 2004). Accordingly, contingent work can call for high-level competencies to which single firms could not conveniently get access to, and contingent workers can be identified as 'consultants' to underline their valuable professional experience (Garsten, 1999).

Technology development supports changes in work processes. The design of digital platforms allows for the social and economic interactions that foster the emergent work arrangements. Airbnb, Etsy, and Upwork are but few examples of virtual marketplaces that have paved the way for imagining, negotiating, and implementing the emergent forms of work (Kenney and Zysman, 2016; Zysman and Kenney, 2017).

One of the consequences of the spread of temporary work is that career pathways have deeply changed; in particular, linear careers made of progressions within a single company are fading away, while protean careers embracing heterogeneous experiences, even apparently inconsistent with each other, become center stage (Caza et al., 2017; Petriglieri et al., 2018, 2019). Individuals frequently engage in multiple jobs simultaneously, not just along the timeline of their working life. Some add a part-time job to their prevalent occupation, while others hold several minor works—the gigs—in parallel (Demetry, 2017; Galperin, 2017; Reilly, 2017). Others yet maintain a regular job while undertaking an entrepreneurial effort: by doing so, they reduce the uncertainty linked to the new initiative and the anxiety related to a possible failure, while postponing a definitive decision on whether to proceed or give up on the new activities (Folta, Delmar, and Wennberg, 2010; Solesvik, 2017).

Heterogeneous forms of contingent work led to the introduction of another popular term: 'slasher' (Alboher, 2007). 'Slasher' refers to individuals who juggle two jobs and therefore, in defining themselves, resort to the slash to express their dualism, e.g., engineer/basketball coach or lawyer/chef. Alboher's book title (*One Person, Multiple Careers*) analyzed the possibility to carry out more jobs and its implications for career management. She provided a large number of stories of 'slashers' who handled multiple work requirements in parallel, be it for necessity or in search of personal fulfillment, and shared the need for incorporating more professional identities into the self-concept. Although the phenomenon of holding more jobs has already been examined from an economic viewpoint (Shishko and Rostker, 1976; Paxson and Sicherman, 1996; Conway and Kimmel, 1998), it is only recently that it has been connected to individual features such as career pathways and professional fulfillment (Arthur, 2008, Caza et al, 2017; Petriglieri et al., 2019). Pursuing plural careers is then becoming a relevant option for workers: according to the US Department of Labor and the Bureau of Labor Statistics (2018), over 7.8 million Americans carried out more than one job simultaneously in the 2016–2017 time span.

The dramatic and manifold changes in work modalities that have been described above have prompted or fostered the diffusion of experiences that resonate with the concept of liminality. Being a contingent worker has been interpreted as a liminal state, in that individuals, be they affiliated with temporary staffing agencies or not, change client companies on a regular basis, thus feeling on the edge of multiple organizations without belonging to any of them (Garsten, 1999; Borg and Söderlund, 2013). Similarly, independent workers like writers, graphic designers, executive coaches, and IT workers have to carve out their own 'holding environment,' as recalled below, to overcome the looming perception of living a liminal experience (Petriglieri et al., 2019). On a related note, plural careerists who are engaged in two different work domains as a means to pursue their inner authenticity may fruitfully turn their being 'betwixt and between' into being 'both one thing and the other,' for instance, both an attorney and a dance teacher or both a doctor and a business owner (Caza et al., 2017).

After a significant body of studies on liminal experiences referring to a variety of work processes have been produced lately, we can identify the most recurrent types that organization and management literature has offered us: Liminality as being at the boundaries of two or more organizations, liminality as contingent work, liminality within a single organization, liminality as the pursuit of a plural careers (Table 2.1). The typologies reported above share the basic assumption of liminality in organization and management studies, i.e., that liminality be a feature of emergent work processes. According to this view, facing a certain situation—for instance, being a consultant or a freelancer working for more clients—implies living a liminal experience. Consulting projects spark liminal experiences,

Table 2.1 Types of organizational liminal experiences

Types of liminality in organization studies	Main characteristics	Instances	Relevant references
Liminality across organizational boundaries	Affiliation with more organizations	Consultants, managers of interorganizational networks, R&D scientists	Zabuski and Barley, (1997); Czarniawska and Mazza (2003)
Liminality as contingent work	Temporary affiliation with an organization	Project workers, temporary workers	Garsten (1999); Barley and Kunda (2004); Borg and Söderlund (2015)
Liminality within an organization	Performance of more roles within an organization	Managers of knowledge-sharing computers, project managers	Swan et al. (2016); Hodgson and Paton (2016)
Liminality as the pursuit of plural careers	Performance of multiple jobs in parallel	'Slashers' (e.g., teachers and writers, lawyers, and chefs)	Alboher (2007); Barker and Caza (2017)

as well as acting as an interorganizational network manager engenders a discourse on liminality: it is the work arrangement that triggers liminality, rather than *how* individuals interpret, negotiate, and enact work under similar circumstances, which might generate different perceptions and experiences of liminality. In the remaining of the chapter, the analysis of the state of the art of organization and management studies on liminality will reflect this common premise which has been eloquently stated by Howard-Grenville, Golden-Biddle, Irwin and Mao (2011, p. 525) as follows: 'although the concept of liminality has been used in organizational studies, it has been treated primarily as a structurally imposed condition by virtue of profession and role.' Conversely, only a limited number of studies have delved into liminality as a consequence of significant events or jolts that subvert a traditional way of acting and interacting without clearly indicating what may come next (O'Loughlin et al., 2017; Jahn, Cornwell, Drengner, and Gaus, 2018).

Liminality across Organizational Boundaries

Operating at the crossroads of different organizations is a prominent work arrangement to which liminality has been applied as interpretive lens in organization studies. Two seminal contributions brought to the fore this situation as potentially liminal, thus paving the way for subsequent exploration: the study on scientists carried out by Zabuski and Barley back in 1997 and the study on consultants carried out by Czarniawska and Mazza in 2003.

In their insightful paper, Zabuski and Barley interpreted scientists affiliated with R&D units as liminars. Through an ethnography conducted on industrial scientists working for the European Space Agency, the Authors showed how researchers reacted against the conflicting imperatives posed by the administrative control exerted by management and the occupational control demanded by the scientific community. While acting as knowledge brokers between their employing company and the community in which relevant knowledge is developed and shared, scientists were expected by management to firmly identify with the former and to keep a cognitive distance from the latter. Four patterns of membership were, however, delineated: a sense of belonging to the firm and of exclusion from the community; a sense of exclusion from the firm and of belonging to the community; a sense of belonging to both collectives; and a sense of exclusion from both collectives. Remarkably, the scientists under study could be traced back to the fourth type: 'they are *liminal* to both the scientific community and the firm' (p. 370, italics in the original). They felt 'neither "bureaucrats" nor "researchers"' (p. 392) and had 'consciousness of difference without consciousness of kind' (p. 394). In this being neither pure scientists nor operative professionals lied their liminal identities, which helped them accommodate managerial requirements with participation in the scientific debate. In the setting under study, inhabiting a 'no man's land' and feeling 'neither here nor there' reduced the drawbacks of liminality, as knowledge flows are fostered on one side, and managerial influence is downplayed, on the other. This significant contribution to liminality in organizations embraced an interpretation of liminality that has characterized most studies on this topic: liminality is associated with a role, such as being an industrial scientist, a hybrid entrepreneur, or a consultant (Sturdy and Wright, 2011; Söderlund and Borg, 2018). In this case, being industrial scientists that do not feel a sense of membership to neither their company nor the collective of scientists implies living a liminal experience, no matter what the individual characteristics and background may be. Unlike the original interpretation elaborated in anthropology, liminality is not bound here to come to an end, unless individuals change their job.

A similar stance applies to research on consultants, who are considered to be liminal as they are simultaneously engaged with the consulting firm and with the client company. In their much-cited paper on consultants, Czarniawska and Mazza (2003) referred to consulting as a liminal space. In this liminal space, various actions and influence have been acknowledged to consultants. They can be regarded as 'parasites': since 'they are in between, neither here nor there but in the middle' (Clegg, Kornberger, and Rhodes, 2004, p. 39), they have the opportunity to acquire knowledge from their clients, elaborate on it, and turn it into tools to be sold to different clients. Still as a consequence of their lying at the boundaries across organizations, consultants can be labeled as 'external irritants' able to stimulate clients' change through the introduction of elements from the outside (Luhmann, 2005; Mohe and Seidl, 2011). Czarniawska-Joerges (1990) and Czarniawska and Mazza (2012) proposed yet a different framing of consultants as 'merchants of meaning' who offer interpretive templates, i.e., a set of tools that are intermingled with each other, allow to look at organizational settings from a different perspective, and bring in changes or, alternatively, confirm the status quo. Whatever the influence exerted by consultants may be, the process of consulting 'can be fruitfully described as the creation of a state of liminality' and consultants 'are condemning themselves to remain in this state—as long as they are occupied with consulting' (Czarniawska and Mazza, 2012, p. 438).

Based on this assumption, studies on consultancy have placed particular emphasis on the rites, ceremonies, and symbols tallying the liminal experience. As anticipated in Chapter 1, the start-up meeting of a project serves as a ritual of incorporation/separation that marks the inclusion of consultants into the client company, while setting regular employees aside from colleagues who are not going to be involved in the project. At this stage, employees take on the role of learners or apprentices. During the project performance, a spoliation ritual is claimed to occur: consultants acknowledge and accept their liminality, thereby giving up on some of their prestige, while client's employees deprive themselves of exclusive competencies concerning their company. When projects approach the end, a new ritual likely unfolds, which consists of separation/incorporation: consultants take gradually distance from the client company, while employees who have participated in the project get prepared to go back to their ordinary tasks and relationships. Rites match symbols and artifacts: the final report that explains the project content and formulates suggestions functions as a 'boundary object' (Bechky, 2003) pointing to a regained demarcation between consultants and the client company's members.

Different rites were investigated by Sturdy, Schwartz, and Spicer (2006). Business meals, such as formal dinners at the client CEO's house and in upscale restaurants, as well as informal events in mid-range restaurants, in which the client CEO, managers, consultants, and the consulting company partners participated, acted as rites to carve out liminal spaces that both consultants and client company members harnessed tactically. Liminal spaces were ambiguous in that they would rule out consolidate routines based on hierarchical relations, while offering insights into both the consulting company and the client company's 'power map.' Those rites helped build an anti-structure, according to Turner's meaning, in which information would flow and be shared openly, and possible strategic initiatives could be raised and made 'politically acceptable' (Sturdy et al., 2006, p. 947) before being presented and discussed in the organizational arena. The liminal spaces sealed by meal-related rituals were ambivalent: they reinforced the nature of the anti-structure, in that they generated alternative rules and routines, such as the choice of the topics to be tackled during conversations or turn-taking in offering drinks, but also mirrored existent power dynamics, such as the relationships between the client CEO and his or her middle managers or between these latter and consultants. In this sense, the anti-structure stemming from business meal-related events can partially subvert social routines and structures, but not dramatically overwrite them. In line with the consequences of liminality highlighted in Chapter 1, liminal spaces can turn out to be unsettling, as happened especially with the client company managers who felt some discomfort in identifying these events as business or leisure time and who struggled to share documents like business plans and charts outside the firm precinct. At the same time, though, the novel norms and ties emerging in the common liminal space enabled the various actors involved to delineate possible scenarios and future courses of action, thereby testifying to the creative potential of liminal experiences.

Within the framework of liminality as being at the crossroads of different organizations, then, founding elements of liminality assume their own nuances. In the case of consultancy, the anti-structure is not in sharp contrast to traditional order, as argued in Turner's studies, but develops alternative rules, norms, and routines. Even more remarkably, rites, ceremonies, and symbols play a major role in the liminal experience, because, unlike former assumptions, they are not intended to signal the beginning, the unfolding, and the end of a given transition, but a likely continuous entering and exiting liminal spaces, as Czarniawska and Mazza (2012, p. 438) stressed: 'Unlike participants in rites of passage, however, consultants do not leave it to reenter later after a completed transition. They travel back and forth, in and out of the liminal spaces.'

Operating at the boundaries across different organizations pertains to managers who run interorganizational relationships, too (Marchington and Vincent, 2004; Tempest and Starkey, 2004; Marchington, Grimshaw, Rubery, and Willmott, 2005). Ellis and Ybema (2010) examined front-line and middle managers in supply chains for agricultural, textile-related, and automotive products. Individuals in charge of network management have to recast themselves continuously to adapt to different audiences (customers, suppliers, colleagues, competitors) through the contraction and expansion of their circle of identification. The oscillation between 'us' and 'them'—suppliers and customers, leaders and non-leaders, or 'in' and 'out'—is handled through four different repertoires. Boundaries can be drawn around organizations to imply what lies inside and outside, specifically to differentiate a company from the marketplace. Boundaries can be also used to mark power relations in the marketplace, i.e., by adopting labels like 'them' for competitors, clients, or suppliers in contrast to 'us' as focal actors. In addition, boundaries can be set around relationships, in which 'us' and 'them' tell who is 'on board' and close from who is distant and potentially threatening among the value chain actors. Finally, boundaries can address marketing management, i.e., identify those who detain expert marketing skills and those who do not, and thus position a myriad of atomized actors. Individuals are endlessly engaged in this repertoire enactment, dwelling in a blurred situation, which led Ellis and Ybema (2010, p. 298) to state that 'identity formation in liminal situations is an inherently dynamic and ambiguous process.' Accordingly, managers of interorganizational relationships can be described as 'boundary bricoleurs' who never reach a long-lasting, clear-cut self-definition. As is recurrent for liminality occurring in organizational settings, repertoires are individual responses without a collective connotation (Box 2.1).

BOX 2.1 THE RHETORIC OF WORKING ON THE EDGE

How do individuals work at the boundaries across a plurality of organizations? Rhetoric seems to be a valuable resource to make sense of brokerage across organizations (Mattarelli, Tagliaventi, Carli, and Gupta, 2017). According to Czarniawska and Mazza (2003), some consultants who felt that they enjoyed scarce autonomy in their operations used the expression 'call-girl,' 'child,' or 'servant' to refer to the necessity to comply with the client companies' expectations and requests and to the pressure to be accountable for time management to which they are subjected. Consultants also feel as if they sometimes had to 'quarrel with themselves' when they are not only suspended between different organizations, but between different roles, too, e.g., Personnel Director and Vice-CEO, and have to play both roles in a same context like a meeting. If being consultant implies living a liminal experience in the studies examined, then consultants are likely to live more liminal experiences in parallel. Perceptions of suspension can vary during a project lifespan, and the same consultants who have stressed their being 'betwixt and between' their employing company and the client company can boast that they are 'la crème de la crème' or the 'genius' able to do the real stuff for client companies. Consultants' rhetoric is not stable, but rather changes from person to person and from project stage to stage. There seems to be no such thing as a single and undifferentiated kind of liminality in consultancy.

Rhetoric helps also managers of interorganizational relationships come to terms with the ambiguity of their position in between different firms. Ellis and Ybema (2011) showed how managers reproduce discursive boundaries, using alternatively 'us' and 'them' and 'internal' and 'external' when referring to the companies with which they interact in the value chain, and can find relief in the use of an inclusive 'everybody' when recounting their work activities. 'Everybody' in fact evokes that they, as managers who 'get their hands dirty' in handling the exchanges among clients and suppliers, are not solitary actors, but members of an organization, although this latter may be one time a client and the other a supplier, in any case mutable over time. These terms are harnessed by different managers to depict similar situations, thus testifying to the nuances and differences from individual to individual that liminal experiences entail.

Liminality as Contingent Work

Forms of contingent work, which have been spreading internationally, as recalled above, have been traditionally associated with liminality. Back in 1999, Garsten used the lens of liminality to examine the benefits and drawbacks of temporary work in particular. Liminality can in fact serve as 'an alternative to work as organized and structured in bureaucratic, industrial organizations; an alternative to regular, full-time employment contracts' (Garsten, 1999, p. 606). Being a 'temp' can be a work condition endowed with different drivers and endpoints: it can be a transient situation in which to test possible pathways and career shifts, while searching for a permanent employment, or it can be an enduring condition from which it becomes difficult to escape or that people may desire to stick to. Some positions are advertised as 'temp-to-perm' to stress their essence as a passage towards stable forms of employment, whereas in other cases, temporary work becomes a long-term perspective

(Borg and Söderlund, 2013, 2015). Working on a project basis for various companies can in fact be an ongoing state that individuals may or may not wish to elude (Borg and Söderlund, 2015): it can be sustained by the desire to be able to take time off for study or travel (Garsten, 1999), keep options open for the future, experiment with possible selves (Ibarra, 2004), pursue self-authenticity at work (Caza et al., 2017), or, conversely, just entail frustration for not finding a suitable permanent position.

Resorting to contingent work can be an ambivalent experience for workers and firms. On one hand, post-industrial organizations gain in flexibility by availing themselves of various types of contingent work (Ahrne, 1994; Garsten, 1999). On the other hand, though, effects on workers are subtler, in line with the liminality consequences analyzed in Chapter 1. Individuals can nourish feelings of substitutability and disposability summed up by Garsten's (1999) expression—'being just a temp'—which implies the perception of being different, perhaps second-level workers compared to permanent workers. Contingent workers often help regular employees with their tasks, ensuring that these latter keep up with their own deadlines and attain satisfying performance, but remain marginal in the client companies' organizational processes (Kunda, 1992). Their activities can unfold in separate spaces, even performed backstage, to reduce opportunities for interaction with regular employees and their intermingling, thus preserving a limited exposure to sources of information about the company (Garsten, 1999). A 'hierarchy of territories' can be organized to this goal: temporary workers are prevented from attending company meetings dealing with core business issues, although their involvement in social events and use of health facilities can happen (Garsten, 1999). The spacelessness that characterize liminality therefore appear to apply to contingent workers' experiences (Kellerman, 2008; Küpers, 2011; Huang, Xiao, and Wang, 2018). On the other hand, however, temporary workers can gain in reflexivity, and enjoy the possibility to monitor and exert control over their own activities, thereby avoiding the hierarchical pressure by which regular employees must instead abide. As Garsten (1999, p. 606) claimed, temporary work can spawn mixed feelings that comprise 'marginality and potency, inferiority and release.'

The role of temporary staffing agencies as brokers between individual workers as liminars and client companies has been highlighted (Garsten, 1999). Agencies aim to act as substitutes for employing companies in two ways. First, they try to promote a shared organizational identity that might serve as a target of identification (Dutton, Dukerich, and Harquail, 1994; Dukerich, Golden, and Shortell, 2002). Second, they engage in the construction of a communitas among temps. With these goals in mind, for instance, they organize social events to bring workers together and distribute newsletters to convey the message that their members are part of an organization which backs them. It is noteworthy that, unlike instances of communitas in anthropology, ties among individuals sharing a similar occupation are mostly efforts on the staffing agencies' side and do not grow spontaneously out of the common work experience as contingent workers. The lack of a sense of 'togetherness' among liminars is claimed by contingent workers who deem the development of a tight-knit communitas as just an illusion (Garsten, 1999): they act as 'threshold people,' aware of living a solitary experience at the edge of organizations (Küpers, 2011). The ambivalence of temporary work arrangements attains to the way staffing agencies operate, too: in spite of their sponsoring organizational identification and commitment, Garsten (1999) made the example of frequent advertisement for 'just-in-time' personnel that celebrated the substitutability of temporary workers for client companies. Regarding this issue, a paradox can be envisaged: temporary work may be sought after in the market because of the sophisticated competencies that it can offer, while the replaceability of these competencies is communicated and traded by staffing agencies.

Another situation evoking liminality in contingent work is that of interim managers who are hired to run operations for a limited time. They feel to be located both within and outside the employing company, called to handle stability and instability at the same time, balancing opposing pushes, in particular when they have to orchestrate dramatic changes that meet strong resistance by regular workers (Goss and Bridson, 1998).

Late research on contingent work has further stressed individual proactivity in making sense of and carving out liminal experiences. Borg and Söderlund (2015) examined conceptions of work and related practices of mobile project workers employed as technical consultants by various client companies. Based upon their study, contingent work emerges as an ongoing condition that does not lead to any future incorporation into permanent work. Three individual interpretations of contingent workers are presented. The first can be traced back to 'work as assignment handling.' According to this view, project workers see their work as a service to project teams established by the client companies: they focus on the tasks assigned to them and remain usually peripheral in decision-making processes, initiating changes only if required by client management. Professionals who embrace this conception of work aim for a 'safe zone' that may allow them to reduce the stress that uncertainty about the future engenders. The 'safe zone' is associated with the possibility to set prolonged relationships with clients. It is only when repeated contracts with few clients are granted that the perception of the negative outcomes of liminality, such as anxiety and frustration, is attenuated. The second emergent conception refers to 'work as a learning platform': contingent work is here seen as a learning opportunity due to project workers' more active role in project execution. They realize that some flexibility is needed, and tasks that go beyond the initial agreement must be performed in order for the project to be completed successfully. It is these additional, unforeseen tasks that enable competence enrichment. Notwithstanding the development of competencies that appeal to mobile project worker and whose achievement is acknowledged by them as well as by the client management, stress and frustration are still felt as a consequence of the liminal situation.

The third work conception regards 'work as knowledge transfer.' In this case, emphasis is placed upon knowledge sharing: on one hand, project workers convey bring highly valued knowledge to client companies, but, on the other, they have the chance of expanding on their knowledge repositories by taking on a proactive role in the project setup. Professionals in fact make independent and spontaneous moves to advance the project, going beyond the original assignments: by doing so, they bring the knowledge and expertise acquired in different settings to the organization at stake, while increasing their own knowledge and expertise. Contingent workers may, in this work view, suggest changes to the project that can impact upon the client's processes also at a business level, gaining a comprehensive perspective on organizational functioning. When work is considered as a knowledge transfer opportunity, the negative consequences of liminality are lessened, and acceptance of fuzziness and vagueness is counterbalanced from the recognition that competencies grow from project to project.

As with the temporary workers studied by Garsten (1999), mobile project workers do not succeed in developing a sense of communitas, though (Borg and Söderlund, 2015). This constitutive element of liminality seems to fade away in empirical evidence collected in organizational settings: liminars act as independent actors, without a strong urge for sharing their experience with fellows. Liminality seems to be as an essentially solitary condition, and this perception is even heightened in temporary, cross-functional teams (Borg and Söderlund, 2013, 2015): the lack of previous collaboration and the weak perspective of working together again in the future impinge upon the willingness to build a community among contingent workers, while ties with the client's regular workers barely exceed mere acquaintance.

It is notable that liminality as contingent work emphasizes the capability to set up individual practices rather than engage in collective practices. Liminal experiences take here on a more individualized nuance than in Turner's accounts: the sense of communitas among peers going through a similar transition seems to be rather replaced by individual agency. Petriglieri et al.'s (2019) study on independent workers shed light on single trajectories to handle liminality from a different perspective. Unlike the temporary workers analyzed by Garsten (1999), independent workers tend to reinforce direct relationships with client companies that are not mediated by third parties like temporary staffing agencies, and to sell their services directly to the market (Ashford, George and Blatt, 2007; Cappelli and Keller, 2013). The 65 independent workers examined by Petriglieri and coauthors (2019) shared the view of organizations as entities that could secure pay and a network of relationships, but whose structure and politics could turn out to be suffocating, which led them to take a distance and opt for independence. As the authors (2019, p. 18) underlined, these independent workers did not feel 'marginal, liminal, or in transition between organizations. They were firmly outside.' Interestingly, a work choice, i.e., being a freelancer, which may resonate with a liminal experience, is not felt this way owing to the very tactics that individuals enact. Specifically, cultivating a personal holding environment safeguards a work identity and reduces the perception of precariousness associated with independent work. A holding environment comprises four types of connections that help cope with the conflicting emotions ensuing from work precariousness, and maintain a high level of productivity that preserves an image of self as competent and energetic worker. The first type of connections refers to the attachment to personal routines. Individuals cultivate their own daily routines that make them remain focused and reduce the stress related to uncertainty about future assignments. Routines can underline the boundaries between work and leisure time activities, with the goal of increasing discipline and attention when performing work activities. To some extent, these routines can be likened to individual rites denoting the entry, permanence, and exit from the work domain. The second type of connections concerns physical spaces. Independent workers acknowledge some spaces, such as a portion of their home or a public library, as workplaces shielding them from distractions and sustaining the productivity that is the core of their working self. The third type of connections is represented by significant people with whom to interact. Individuals resort to friends, relatives, old classmates, or counselors for reassurance and encouragement. The fourth and final connection links freelancers to a broader purpose. Purpose can lie in the importance to listen to one's inner self instead of surrendering to external expectations (e.g., tending to a long-term, safe occupation), in the alignment between personal fulfillment and superordinate goals (e.g., the realization that individual choices resonate with the American culture embodying freedom and creativity), or in the conviction to select only appointments that may bring a valuable contribution to the world. Through these different types of connections, holding environments serve to secure the sense of an industrious self in the wake of independent work fluctuations. By building an environment that is perceived as protective and conducive to satisfactory performance over time, independent workers in fact experience a 'tolerable and generative precariousness' (Petriglieri et al., 2019, p. 156). As a consequence of individual courses of action then, a situation that could spawn a perception of liminality emphasized instead its characteristic as voluntary choice to resist the control and pressure exerted by organizational contexts. While individual agency turns a potentially liminal experience into a regular work-like arrangement, social bonding with individuals making similar work choices once more fades away: upholding links are developed with a range of actors, but no communitas is detected among freelancers (Box 2.2).

BOX 2.2 FOCUS ON LIMINAL EXPERIENCES AND CONTINGENT WORK

Qualitative research on temporary workers throws a light on how individuals cope with a working life that has been framed as liminal in the literature. The seminal book by Barley and Kunda (2004) told the stories of technical contractors that underline their different motivations, pathways, sentiments, and responses to the choice to become contingent workers in the Silicon Valley.

Contingent work emerges, in the singular life histories, as a twofold arrangement, in which one and the same aspect (time management, compensation, learning opportunities, flexibility, autonomy, social relationships) is markedly imbued with light and shade, alongside impressive variations across individuals.

The three stories that open the book well account for individual differences in undertaking and managing a life as independent contractor. Kent is a highly skilled computer scientist who turned to technical consulting after a long experience as a full-time employee in different companies that caused him a burnout. He has embraced and mostly appreciates his experience as a freelance, shifting companies every six to eight months and enjoying spare time to cultivate his personal passions. Although he relies on a network of acquaintances and colleagues to find new appointments and reduce downtime, i.e., periods between contracts, he testifies to a solitary effort in which he strives to cooperate with client companies' less experienced members and interacts with users' groups almost exclusively to further public recognition and improve attractiveness in the market.

A different trajectory pertains to Yolanda, who originally was a secretary that gradually turned into an IT technician through a training on the job focused on problem-solving. Learning is her obsession: she surfs the net, looks up specialized magazines, and reads technical books to increase her competencies. She is linked to staffing agencies to assist her in searching for client companies because she does not avail herself of an extensive network of ties yet, but she chooses contracts based on their learning potential. When asked about the reason why she has quit long-term employment, she replies that she looks for higher wages, more independence, and less organizational politics.

Finally, Julian tells yet another story in comparison with Kent and Yolanda. He resorted to independent contracting after a series of layoffs basically because he could not find a satisfactory permanent job, but that remains the safe harbor he longs for. As a matter of fact, he has been moving back and forth between permanent and temporary job arrangements, since he cannot give up on the idea of belonging to an organization that reciprocates his commitment. Downtime prompts a deep sense of fragility and discomfort to him. Like Yolanda, he feels unsecure without the support of staffing agencies,

(Continued)

and unlike Kent, he likes being involved in professional communities for the sake of sharing experiences and feeling some kinship rather than reinforcing his professional profile.

The three trajectories summed up above point to different liminal experiences within the same work format, but with a unifying thread: going against the mainstream of sticking to a full-time job with a reliable employer only. This orientation makes them all 'unlikely rebels,' albeit of dissimilar types.

Liminality within a Single Organization

Liminality does not only unfold at the boundaries across organizations, but also within organizations. Various experiences of liminality have been reported to occur in the traditional settings offered by firms and within the framework provided by permanent jobs. A first type of liminality within a single organization refers to the roles held. A relevant study addressing liminality in these circumstances was carried out by Swan, Scarbrough and Ziebro (2016). They examined 43 managers who took on responsibility as knowledge-sharing community coordinators in addition to their jobs within a department or function. The assumption that they be liminars is based upon the observation that 'knowledge-sharing community coordinators had roles with characteristics typical of liminal positions, including a lack of standardized job titles or, in some cases, any formal title whatsoever.' (p. 787). Performing a new part-time role, while still continuing with usual tasks, is deemed to be a liminal state that individuals manage through individual practices, similarly to what observed for independent workers' holding environment.

The emergent tactics to handle an additional role can be traced back to front-stage and back-stage practices. Front-stage practices target senior management and are aimed at raising their awareness and getting their support: recurrent actions imply advocating the community, i.e., promoting the necessity of communities for the achievement of organizational goals, and documenting outputs, i.e., providing evidence of community usage and successes. Conversely, back-stage practices address community members and are mostly unknown to senior management: identifying potential members and trying to get them onboard (developing membership), contributing directly to the community functioning, and sponsoring other members' contributions (facilitating engagement) are instances of these practices. Finally, stewardship practices serve both front-stage and back-stage purposes by trying to reconcile groups' divergent expectations and needs through the definition and adjustment of the objectives pursued.

In spite of playing out these practices, some managers' accounts are still interpreted by Swan et al. (2016) as examples of liminality: in telling their stories in fact these managers talk about the vague nature and the lack of focus of their job, which are likened to an experience of liminality. Under these circumstances, the liminality acknowledged to managers engenders creative agency in role enactment, as it allows for greater flexibility in performing tasks and establishing relationships. Individual patterns of role enactment as community coordinators can be identified as knowledge brokers, who prompt and sustain community members' knowledge exchanges; internal consultants, who imbue communities with strategic tools and performance measurements; avant-garde, who advocate for the community development in light of his or her own objectives, such as getting visibility; service provider, who develops the community services to help achieve organizational goals; and finally, the orphaned child, who is active in the community, but feels abandoned by management and isolated. Although the power of creative agency varies across the above role enactments, with knowledge brokers and internal consultants having the highest potential, liminality stemming from a double position frees imagination and proactivity. Remarkably, it is individual tactics that are underlined both in front-end and back-stage practices: no sense of community is recorded among coordinators, in spite of their common focus on combing community management with functional roles.

Another kind of liminality within a single organization related to the enactment of more roles is that of internal consultants (Wright, 2009). Managers who act as internal consultants can be interpreted as liminars since they hold an 'ambiguous organizational location, being permanent employees but also operating outside the traditional activities and structures of the business organization' (Wright, 2009, p. 310). In this situation, as in the case of more roles just discussed, individual reactions take center stage and revolve around identity work. Managers build various identities to handle ambiguity, ranging from 'trusted adviser' who offer the expert's competencies to colleagues in need, to 'service provider,' willing to solve routine problems upon colleagues' demand, to social 'outcast,' rejected by, and in contrast to, the prevailing organizational culture. Identity work is played out to foster 'a strongly positive self-identity, denoting autonomy and an ability to cross internal structural boundaries' (p. 314). Like knowledge community coordinators, managers serving as internal consultants do not undertake any collective action; theirs is still an example of solitary effort to face liminality.

Liminality within an organization can also be linked to stable affiliation with a company and prevalent operations within its premises, while holding deeply valued connections with other organizations. Project managers are specimen of this form of liminal experiences. They are considered to be 'caught in the middle' as they are involved in a double source of liminality: that of transitioning from a technical specialist role to a managerial role, and that of feeling at a crossroads between the employing organization and the professional community (Hodgson and Paton, 2016). Project managers in fact face the transition from carrying out project activities firsthand to organizing and coordinating project resources, which is deemed as a former type of liminal experience (liminality between technical and managerial position). At the same time, they are affiliated to an employing company, usually a big enterprise, but feel loyal to their profession, in particular to the community of practice built among project managers around the world (liminality between local and cosmopolitan professional). This latter situation resonates with the experience of scientists who feel a sense of belonging both to the company whose R&D unit they work for and to the scientific community they interact with (Zabuski and Barley, 1997). Dual liminality is addressed by project managers through identity work based on dialectics: they engage in discourses that can be antithetical (e.g., prioritizing external over internal knowledge or the reverse; advocating for the universality of technical knowledge and skills or, on the contrary, for the relevance of organizational process expertise). Discourses can also reconcile contrasting perspectives, as happens when professionals claim that proficiency in project management can help them adapt to heterogeneous organizational contexts, thereby bringing together the technical and managerial perspectives, or that participation in professional communities leads them to better respond to organizational needs, thus integrating the cosmopolitan and local perspectives. Be dual liminality handled through juxtaposition or reconciliation, it is worth stressing that individual identity work can spur tensions among professionals, as Hodgson and Paton (2016, p. 35) claimed: 'What is striking, then, is the breadth of positions adopted within what is implicitly the same role, and the resultant tensions and conflicts between fellow PMs [project managers] themselves.' Contacts among project managers driven by common interests and similar competencies therefore differ substantially from the ties characterizing communitas ties: misunderstandings or even divergencies can prevail over a sense of closeness and affinity.

Finally, liminality within an organization has been attributed to career transitions within a company. Individuals undergoing promotions from one position to another or the transfer from one unit to another deal with the experience of dwelling in a 'gray area,' being unsure about the duties and patterns of interactions that the new role may require. Ibarra (1999) provided an effective description of the uncertainty and the challenges that workers handling career moves have to cope with: in particular, she underlined the intense identity work that, under these circumstances, individuals have to go through to adapt to a significant professional change. Although Ibarra's work did not explicitly mention liminality, the transition she described bears some similarities with the passages that underlie the liminality construct. In light of career advancements and new roles, individuals in fact lose their previous references and embark on intensive identity work to figure out who they can become in the new role. The trajectory highlighted in this study unravels how individuals first observe role models that may act as an inspiration to approach the new tasks and requirements. They then try on 'provisional selves' that pave the way for realizing who they might become in their role: they can replicate role models' behaviors, styles, and attitudes or adopt 'true-to-self' strategies that evoke authenticity rather than imitation of others. 'Provisional selves' function as possible selves to be tested, experimented, and eventually adopted, modified, or rejected. In the third and final phase, 'provisional selves' are gauged according to internal standards, especially congruence between the worker's public persona and his or her inner aspirations, and according to external feedback that may validate the evolution, fail to sustain it, or provide hints about how to adapt it.

In a similar vein, organizational entries and exits, promotions, transfers, and demotions, intra-organizational moves, all represent passages in which individuals take a distance from previously held role, routines, and established interactions to approach a new set of duties and expectations (Louis, 1980, 1982; Ebaugh and Ebaugh, 1988; Haski-Leventhal and Bargal, 2008). Also training programs preparing workers for new responsibilities can resonate with liminality, as they entail a transition from long-held competencies and courses of action to new scenarios. This holds particularly true when managers are concerned, since they can have a greater impact on organizational decision-making processes and therefore trigger further liminal experiences involving co-workers (Eriksson-Zetterquist, 2002; Dubouloy, 2004).

All the configurations recalled above—performance of more than one role in the same setting, oscillating between technical and managerial roles, role transitions—position liminality within organizations, not between organizations. Küpers (2011, p. 49) meaningfully expressed the nature of liminal experience developing in organizations by stating that 'liminality is not outside or peripheral to organisation and leadership, but in the cracks within its very social structure and processes' (Box 2.3).

BOX 2.3 FOCUS ON LIMINAL EXPERIENCES WITHIN AN ORGANIZATION

Individuals can feel 'neither here nor there' even when they belong to a single organization. A perception of suspension may pertain to workers who take on more roles within a company: in spite of a well-defined affiliation to the employing firm, their situation can be likened to those who operate across more firms.

Swan et al. (2016) provided some good excerpts from the interviews to coordinators of knowledge-sharing communities that unveil individual motivations, attitudes, and concerns. These communities are mostly aimed at improving organizational processes, sharing best practices, and developing professional competencies. Individuals differ in their attitudes towards community management: for instance, Martin saw them as a privileged internal 'marketplace' in which to exchange knowledge and enhance skills that should appeal to all professionals, whereas Aubrey and Robert were worried about how to keep community members committed in the long run, beyond the initial interest for a new initiative, if participation is not deemed to be conducive to some appealing outcomes.

Heterogeneity of interpretations of community scope and effectiveness are echoed in the way managers react against the overlapping of community coordination with their ordinary tasks in the departments they are affiliated to, which underlies their liminal experience. For some of them, the ambiguity of the role of community manager allows for individual proactivity that reduces the perception of being 'betwixt and between': Steve and Aubrey, for instance, split their time between the regular work to be performed and community coordination, which was left for the evenings and weekends. It is arguable that the perception of indeterminateness is reduced, in these cases, by the capacity to set boundaries between time and space pertaining to different roles, likely weakening sensations of timelessness and spacelessness. Conversely, others, such as Esther and John, struggled to realize how to combine their different roles due to the lack of clear focus and specifications. They ended up feeling stuck in the middle between their usual work activities and coordination obligations, feeling puzzled and uncertain about what actions to take and who they might turn out to be as professionals in the end. It is worthwhile stressing how individuals can make sense and enact additional roles—namely, organizational unit manager and knowledge community coordinator—differently in a same setting and therefore differently feel to be engaged in a transition and liminal.

Liminality as the Pursuit of Multiple Careers

The recent evolution of work processes that is the starting point of this chapter has been supporting the pursuit of multiple careers in light of the search for authenticity and self-fulfillment, not just for economic reasons (Yagil and Medler-Liraz, 2013; Hewlin, Dumaz, and Burnett, 2017). Although the enactment of more jobs, called 'moonlighting,' was originally rooted in the need to complement the primary source of income (e.g., Krishnan, 1990; Averett, 2001), individuals have been increasingly resorting to this work choice to foster skills development, reinforce flexibility, and nourish passion for what they do (e.g., Hipple, 2010; Lalé, 2015).

Simultaneously performing and identifying with more jobs is becoming the 'new normal' (Waldorf, 2016). An increasing number of people in fact engage in work activities that involve more groups, professions, or jobs (Sliter and Boyd, 2014; Ramarajan, Rothbard, and Wilk, 2017). The 'slashers,' who define who they are by tending to two or more occupations, are on the rise: individuals working as chefs and lawyers or as accountants and cartoonists account for their parallel employment by calling into question the necessity to complement income, but especially the possibility to become more skilled and find more job satisfaction (Alboher, 2007). Identity theorists have long posited that the self may be multi-dimensional, comprising different identities related to multiple job holding or social affiliations (e.g., Stryker and Burke, 2000; Burke and Stets, 2009). The observation that careers have become 'protean,' continuously morphing, in the pursuit of coherence between 'who one is' and 'what one does,' not necessarily in a single domain (Pratt, Rockmann, and Kaufmann, 2006; Caza, Vough, and Puranik, 2018), can be framed within this stance.

Pursuing multiple careers can show similarities with a liminal experience. Individuals undertaking more than one job to attain authenticity are often driven by the desire to reach consistency and unification between the different aspects of self, for instance, being a creative artist and an accomplished school teacher (Ashforth and Tomiuk, 2000). The enactment of different elements of the self-view, however, may require to be active in different domains, with heterogenous role tasks and patterns of interaction at play (Ashforth and Tomiuk, 2000): multiple jobholders may struggle to reconcile expectations linked to the aspiration to realize their true self, and the risk of feeling 'caught in the middle' or 'neither here nor there' is therefore likely high. The study by Caza et al. (2017) shed light on how workers may succeed in resolving discrepancies and contradictions among different work identities. Multiple careerists were shown to first play out a 'synchronizing' tactic: they tried to concentrate on the challenges posed by each work role separately, without looking for connections across the different jobs. Only subsequently did they carry out a 'harmonizing' tactic through which they authenticated their self by grasping and stressing the intertwining of different roles. Interestingly, individuals who stick to this pathway did not appear to feel the sensation of being 'betwixt and between' that is the essence of liminality: the puzzlement that initially pertained to their experience as multiple jobholders was in fact overcome through their effort to set linkages across work identities. Once again, as for the independent workers investigated by Petriglieri et al. (2019), the way to live with a possible liminal experience resides in the resort to individual tactics. Even though tactics emerge as common courses of actions similarly implemented by different multiple careerists (e.g., attorney and photographer, writer and musician, childcare educator and fashion designer), they are nonetheless individual responses to the 'feeling-me' challenge. No shared intent and no joint sensemaking pertains to the stories of multiple jobholders that were told in this empirical research.

Another type of multiple careers that can be traced back to liminality concerns hybrid entrepreneurship. Hybrid entrepreneurship can be defined as the performance of entrepreneurial activities as a complement to established work activities (Schulz, Urbig, and Procher, 2016; Demetry, 2017). Hybrid entrepreneurs are in fact 'Individuals who engage in self-employment activity while simultaneously holding a primary job in wage work' (Folta et al., 2010, p. 255). It is noteworthy that entrepreneurship has been argued to be gradually moving away from an 'all or nothing' business to become an integrative pathway driven by a diversification rationale (McGinnis, 2016). Two main rationales are reported to underpin this choice. The former is related to entrepreneurship and lies in the assumption that entry barriers may be perceived to be lower thanks to the expertise gained in the regular work domain. The latter tackles self-realization and resonates with multiple career orientation in general: through their commitment to the creation of a new venture, individuals enjoy more freedom in the realization of their dreams and appropriate more responsibilities over their life (Krueger, Reilly, and Carsrud, 2000; Fauchart and Gruber, 2011). Hybrid entrepreneurship is quite frequent in academia, where researchers can launch spin-offs to commercialize their research outcomes and develop a hybrid identity as academic entrepreneurs (Jain, George, and Maltarich, 2009; Karhunen, Olimpieva, and Hytti, 2017). Remarkably, opportunities to undertake entrepreneurial activities as additional occupation are sustained by the diffusion of the new digital platforms that reduce the need for large-scale assets to reach potential clients (Cohen, 2002).

Hybrid entrepreneurship implies the management of a dual commitment, which can be as fruitful and gratifying as it can spark stress and puzzlement (Joy, 2009; Murray, 2010). Handling different work domains can in fact convey chances for self-fulfillment through the exposure to different stimuli, but requires also the ability to balance competing demands and to resort to reliable cognitive and affective resources (Thorgren, Nordström, and Wincent, 2014; Thorgren, Sirén, Nordström, and Wincent, 2016; Solesvik, 2017). If the tension between self-expression and uncertainty characterizes multiple jobholding overall, in the case of hybrid entrepreneurship finding an equilibrium can be particularly troublesome. The clarity and consistency of entrepreneurs' stories and reputation are in fact of the utmost importance to earn legitimacy and institutional support (Manigart, Wright, Robbie, Desbrières, and De Waele, 1997; Navis and Glynn, 2011). Continuously shifting domains to carry out different jobs may put at stake hybrid entrepreneurs' credibility and lessen their likelihood to obtain funding and social endorsement.

Faced with their dwelling in-between different work roles, nascent entrepreneurs can either move to one of them, giving up on the other, or decide to remain in this situation. The literature on hybrid entrepreneurship has stressed how keeping the previous job while undertaking the new venture can represent a learning space in which to try out and refine the business idea, or, as Folta et al. (2010, p. 256) wrote, 'test the entrepreneurial waters.' Starting with hybrid entrepreneurship is even considered beneficial to the success of the new initiative, since it can act as an incubator backing the development of the business idea (Petrova, 2012; Raffiee and Feng, 2014; Schultz, 2018).

Hybrid entrepreneurs' in-betweenness opens the debate about future courses of action to be taken. From one point of view, entrepreneurs are expected to limit the duration of their dual experience to fully embrace the new venture. This evolution is rooted in the belief that individuals in this situation are willing to pursue what they are most passionate about, i.e., the new idea implementation, as soon as they have the opportunity to switch to full-time self-employment (Folta et al., 2010; Petrova, 2012). Especially in knowledge-intensive industries, the development of a new business is expected to require a total commitment by the entrepreneur(s) (Folta et al., 2010). This endpoint of the hybrid entrepreneur experience resonates with the traditional interpretation of liminality as being temporarily 'neither here nor there' (Turner, 1969; Cook-Sather, 2006; Karioris, 2016; Sleight, 2016). Continuing to perform the previous job, while developing the new idea, appears in this perspective as just a stage of transition towards a future, more definitive state that leaves the previous occupation behind.

Other studies yet have draise the possibility that individuals may become passionate about the very in-betweenness that hybrid entrepreneurship entails. They can appreciate the fact of holding both an entrepreneurial role and a non-entrepreneurial role, benefiting from the interplay between the resources, relationships, and knowledge accessible in the two work spheres (Huyghe, Knockaert, and Obschonka, 2016). As a consequence of the enjoyment of both work spheres, under these circumstances people are not eager to quit their established job, but rather to exploit the positive effect that the two engagements mutually exert on each other (Cohen, 2002; Thorgren et al., 2014). Thorgren et al. (2016) outlined clearly this possibility in their model, referring to the 'maintain the status quo' option as an outcome of hybrid entrepreneurship, while the other two options are a withdrawal from entrepreneurship to rely on the former job only, and total adherence to the new venture, quitting the previous job. Solesvik (2017) advanced this point further by disclosing, through a comparative case study, the contrasting feelings that hybrid entrepreneurs may have vis-à-vis holding another job in addition to launching the new initiative: some of them actually relished the chance to have a better status and nurture their interests in different fields. According to this stance, in-betweenness is interpreted as being 'both here and there' (Garcia-Lorenzo et al., 2018): the synergy between different occupations prevails over potential conflicts ensuing from dual commitment, thus paving the way for a permanence over time of hybrid entrepreneurship arrangements. While hybrid entrepreneurship turning into full-time self-employment echoes with liminality as a stage of passage and with its core features that have been recalled in Chapter 1, identifying with two targets simultaneously—the new venture and the former job—is in line with the latest framing of liminality as a possibly enduring experience. When liminality becomes long-lasting, it can lead individuals to the perception of twofold belongingness, i.e., being people 'who live their lives permanently suspended between two cultural worlds, who identify with both cultural identities and define themselves as "both"' (Ibarra and Obodaru, 2016, p. 54). In Chapter 3, the emergent view of liminality as permanent will be fleshed out in greater depth (Box 2.4).

BOX 2.4 FOCUS ON LIMINAL EXPERIENCES AND MULTIPLE CAREERS

Pursuing more jobs simultaneously can be a state prompting liminal experiences. Individuals in fact assign their time, effort, and psychosocial resources to more than one job, increasing the chances of feeling 'stuck in the middle,' neither completely focusing on one domain nor on the other. This might happen especially when the choice to carry out more than one job ensues from the necessity to increase the overall income or is considered just a temporary phase in a transition towards a stable arrangement in a single domain.

(Continued)

The exhaustive study by Caza et al. (2017) on individuals endeavoring to attain self-authenticity at work showed how this powerful motivator was able to inspire actions that reduced or inhibited the feeling of being 'betwixt and between' two domains. It is the very enactment of plural callings through various tactics in fact that, by enabling individuals to become who they feel to be, seem to rule out the sense of suspension typical of a liminal experience. If this is the common thread linking the stories told in this research, individuals' tension towards plural careers are fairly different. Brittney felt the urge to fill a void; Rose sought to achieve intellectual, physical, and emotional satisfaction when working; Brenda, somewhat confusingly, perceived to have different thrusts inside her (being a doctor, a business owner, an expert). In these three cases, engaging in more jobs represented the only way to feel true to oneself. Other instances yet seemed to bring up a greater likelihood of liminality. For instance, Jeanne declared to struggle to juggle her various aspirations as community college professor, children's book author, and soap opera writer, ending up seeing herself as 'jack of all trades, master of none.' Similarly, Jack and Eliza stated that they believed to be suffering from the imposter syndrome and to commit fraud from time to time when trying to nourish different passions and cultivate heterogeneous interests, without being able to tackle any of them in depth. The possibility of plural careers to trigger liminal experiences undoubtedly deserves more elucidation to highlight the interplat between different rationales to embrace a multiple job perspective, the individual and social dynamics involved, and their aftermath.

Liminality in Specific Organizational Settings

The situations parsed out above testify to the emergence of liminality as an interpretive lens of a variety of work arrangements that have been spreading over the past years. Beyond work processes, other situations have been acknowledged and framed as instances of liminality, principally entrepreneurship and team functioning. The following paragraphs will tap into these applications of the construct of liminality in the organizational field.

Entrepreneurship as Liminal Experience

In addition to hybrid entrepreneurship being regarded as a liminal experience, entrepreneurship itself has been interpreted though the liminality lens in the literature. Henfridsson and Yoo (2013) analyzed trajectory shifts of institutional entrepreneurs, i.e., individuals who are able to create new institutions or to transform extant ones—Thomas Edison or Steve Jobs can be cited as examples—as they are 'actors positioning themselves in the ambiguities emerging from the past-future tension' (p. 932). Trajectory shifts refer to the conception and development of a new innovation pathway: they can wind up reinforcing the initial idea further and moving it towards its implementation or, on the opposite, lead to its failure and abandonment. Henfridsson and Yoo (2014, p. 945) identified trajectory shifts as contexts for liminality due to 'the state of ambiguity faced by institutional entrepreneurs when their new possible innovation trajectory is not fully formed but coexists side by side with established trajectories.' In this study, the authors attribute liminality to the space and time in which a new innovation pathway is conceived of, elaborated, and tested by entrepreneurs, with conventional trajectories being still dominant and difficult to subvert.

The work by Garcia-Lorenzo et al. (2018) addressed nascent necessity entrepreneurs instead. These latter are defined as individuals who are involved in a not yet operating start-up for at least three months mostly out of necessity, such as the lack of alternative employment due to an economic downturn. From this perspective, 'entrepreneurship is ultimately a liminal, transformative condition, a process of creating possible futures and states of being,' (Garcia-Lorenzo et al., 2018, p. 377). In telling the stories of Spanish, British, and Irish unemployed or underemployed people who started new initiatives, these scholars underlined the identity process that is involved in the passage from a condition of a lack of job or unsatisfying job to the birth and growth of a new venture. Liminality is used as an interpretive lens to make sense of nascent entrepreneurs' accounts as they carve out the process of becoming: when new ideas are tested, implemented, and refined, individuals deconstruct, revise, and reconstruct their identity. Living the transition from a currently held job or from unemployment towards the realization of a new company flows in parallel with identity work to forge new self-views. The process of construction of a new occupation and related identity work ensue in circles throughout the entrepreneurial journey, with emergent work opportunities, different sets of relationships, and alternative self-views intertwining with each other. Interestingly, this study on nascent entrepreneurship abides by some of the core characteristics of liminal experiences that have been examined in Chapter 1. First, the revision of the self-view resonates with identity play: in the suspension between a past work (or non-work) situation and a prospective venture to set up, individuals imagine, test, modify, quit, or embrace possible selves (Ibarra and Obodaru, 2016). Identity play does not happen in isolation, but is inspired and reinforced by the strong ties that develop among nascent entrepreneurs. A community in fact comes to light, carrying with it the features of a liminal communitas: previous status and privileges fade, while an egalitarian stance prevails among people who, although originating from heterogeneous backgrounds, share the same aspiration towards a better work future. Feelings of mutual empathy and closeness link nascent entrepreneurs at a time of austerity, as they employ their psychosocial resources to help each other envisage possible selves and are sustained in a similar effort. For most nascent entrepreneurs, the journey ends up with what Garcia-Lorenzo et al. (2018) called a 'reaggregation.' Individuals attain a renewed sense of self alongside, and nested within, a new work context: a 'rewriting' of the self as would-be entrepreneurs represents the outcome of the transition. Reaggregating identity and work context does not mean going back to the old 'normal,' but seizing the opportunities to become someone different in a different space. It is worth stressing that this research offers singular evidence of collective dynamics in organizational studies on liminality, which have been otherwise surprisingly silent thus far to this regard.

Not all individuals starting the entrepreneurial journey culminate with a reaggregation of the self and the work context: some of them remain lost in transition, precisely as they are not capable of building the tight relationships that prompt and sustain creativity. Liminoids, as they are called according to Turner (1974a), are disconnected and alienated from others, and therefore find it harder to finalize their liminal experience.

Liminality has been attributed to entrepreneurs who start home-based online business ventures, too (Di Domenico, Daniel, and Nunan, 2014). Home-based online business entrepreneurs are self-employed people who use their own houses and resources to manage their business. 'Mental mobility' is proposed as a construct able to shed light on how these entrepreneurs handle a liminal experience that involve different spaces. 'Mental mobility' is defined as

> the process through which individuals navigate the liminal spaces between the physical and digital spheres of work, and the overlapping home/workplace, enabling them to manipulate and partially reconcile the spatial, temporal and emotional tensions that are present in such work environments.
>
> (Di Domenico et al., 2014, p. 266)

In an age in which demarcation between home and workplace is getting blurred (Jones and Spicer, 2005, 2009; Fogarty, Scott, and Williams, 2011), individuals have to incessantly navigate the boundaries between home as physical space acting also as workplace and technology as virtual space that enables work to be performed and transferred to users. Liminality resides in the very moving across two different spheres: a physical one and a digital one. The continuous transition between these two spheres is depicted as an experience of ambiguous locating; consequently, liminality is evoked as a suitable interpretive lens. While other locations, such as coffee shops, libraries, and meeting places, are occasionally occupied to complement home as physical spaces, reinforcing the overall ambiguity of the workplace, home is, in the entrepreneurs' accounts, their 'base' or 'central command.' Home becomes a space of (physical) isolation and (virtual) connectedness at the same time, both liberating and constraining individuals, ultimately representing a paradox that one needs to come to terms with. The entrepreneurial initiative is therefore simultaneously edifying and troublesome. The capability to switch from a virtual to a tangible work environment, and from a view of home as a personal life setting to a view of it as the office, and back, is the cognitive resource that allows individuals to cope with ambiguity. Developing a 'mental mobility' emerges as a tactic that individuals resort to in order to handle liminality, overcoming the tension due to the duality of home as comfortable shelter and work arena, or even neither one thing nor the other anymore. As Di Domenico and coauthors underlined in their paper (2018, p. 278), 'Their [entrepreneurs'] apparent relative physical immobility is thus rendered *emotionally and mentally mobile* through daily virtual practices and communications that enable them to reconcile tensions' [italics in the original]. It has to be underlined that, as with hybrid entrepreneurship, different endpoints can be envisaged: the ability to navigate boundaries can be the way to tackle a short-lived experience, bound to turn into a clearer situation in which home and workspace are finally separate locations, or, alternatively, lead to a long-term perspective. As will be detailed in Chapter 3, the likelihood of liminality to quit its temporary nature and assume a permanent stance can be gleaned from this study. It can be noted as well that entrepreneurship is conceptually attributed by the researchers to a situation of tensions and ambiguity resonating with liminality. As Di Domenico and coauthors acknowledge on p. 267, entrepreneurs are 'arguably 'liminal' actors,' which leaves the reader with the reasonable doubt whether they do *actually* feel liminal (Box 2.5).

BOX 2.5 FOCUS ON LIMINAL EXPERIENCES IN ENTREPRENEURSHIP

Engagement in new ventures stands for a fertile setting to explore individual-level dynamics related to liminality. If the new ventures are launched and run while preserving another job, opening up business initiatives may in fact embody a transition with an uncertain endpoint, which could be a total embracement of self-employment or its dismissal. This situation has been accounted for in terms of liminality. Stories of hybrid and nascent entrepreneurship disclose that drivers and sensemaking significantly differ for individuals who embark on this course of action (Garcia-Lorenzo et al., 2018). In recounting their trajectories, some nascent entrepreneurs explain their choice in terms of fit with personality traits, while others underscore their talent in delineating and grasping opportunities, thus downgrading the relevance of potential failure. Faced with the permeability of the context that is being constructed and negotiated with heterogeneous institutional actors, individuals unveil varying abilities to navigate the system, let go of previous taken-for-granted assumptions, and build practices to reinforce their psychosocial resources. Different patterns of action and interaction once the new venture is implemented lead to feelings of confidence and positivity or, conversely, of burnout about the transition itself and its future outcomes, with entrepreneurial narratives being, respectively, more or less defined and articulated. Once again, therefore, similar initiatives of hybrid or nascent entrepreneurship undertaken by apparently comparable actors spark different liminal experiences (or even none at all).

Liminality in Teams and the Relevance of Leadership

The topic of liminality has emerged in research on teams. A distinguished example of liminality in this context is offered by Tempest, Starkey, and Ennew's (2007) study on the disastrous expedition on Mount Everest occurred on May 10, 1996. On that day, several teams of climbers, guides, and clients were surprised by a storm at a high altitude while attempting to descend from summit of Everest towards the Base Camp. Eight of them died, included two expert leaders, and many others were severely injured. While various explanations for this accident had been elaborated in the scientific literature and in the more far-reaching press, Tempest and coauthors adopted a liminality framework to tap into how managerial practices failed to cope with extreme situations and should have been rearranged in what is likened to a Death Zone, i.e., an area in which the human body is unable to survive due to the adverse conditions. Even robust managerial practices, according to the authors' argument, display their limits in liminal conditions. In the case under study, consolidated practices crashed when applied to team members' liminal individuality. Participants in the 1996 Everest expedition were leisure climbers removed from their normal life, spaces, habits, and interactions: they were scarcely interconnected and relatively inexperienced. The analysis brings to the fore four managerial practices that broke down in the wake of liminality in a highly vulnerable setting, and proposes issues to be considered to increase organizations' resilience when extreme conditions are coupled with liminality. A first practice that may turn out to be unsuccessful under similar circumstances regards the resort to temporary organizational forms like contingent work. While organizations may benefit from the flexibility offered by these work arrangements, they may also become exposed to an excess of individualism. Consequently, responsibility over oneself and the others wanes, endangering people and groups. In the Himalaya incident, group members were disconnected and did not care for each other, as they were strangers sharing only the adventure that they were living. To counterbalance individualism, organizations have to foster individual and collective learning through team building techniques, and convey formal support to knowledge sharing.

Strategic intent is another managerial practice that can be impaired by liminality in a risky situation. Although a clear and challenging goal can be a powerful motivator able to leverage scarce resources and drive attention towards its attainment, it can also lead to overemphasize opportunities and neglect threats and points of weakness. The Himalaya climbers were so focused on reaching the summit that they did not pay enough attention to the bigger difficulties that the descent would entail, underestimating the relevance of temperature, weather, and tiredness. To deal with this limit, organizations should maintain and sustain realism in making decisions, always taking into account potential risks and benefits related to any courses of action.

A third managerial practice that may be compromised by liminality in extreme conditions refers to competence growth. Competencies enable organizations to arrange their resources so as to develop products and serve markets effectively (e.g., Grant, 1996). In stressful times, however, competencies can bolster boldness about individual skills, with false assumptions about one's own as well as colleagues' abilities. Inappropriate, even dangerous actions can derive from bravery, and organizations should keep the discourse on the nature of competencies alive. In particular, whether liminars' competencies are well known to coworkers—in the Everest disaster, nobody was aware of what expedition mates really were able to do in the adventure they had embarked on—and whether available competencies are sufficient to face challenging novelties are issues that deserve special attention. Accordingly, time should be devoted to build a mutual understanding among liminars before starting any joint enterprise.

Finally, exerting strategic leadership represents a practice that may bring advantages on an ordinary basis, but become counterproductive when unexpected events occur. A clear strategic leadership in fact can provide a mission and support towards goal achievement, but also spur followers' excessive dependence on guidance and lack of self-reliance. In the Everest case, the two leaders enjoyed a quasi-mythical status: they were believed to be almost invincible 'adventure heroes.' When they, albeit for different reasons, both exceeded their limits and lost control, team members experienced a total puzzlement. Paradoxically, the more impaired leaders became, the more team members relied on them to save their own lives. Deeply stressed out, liminars were not able to trust each other and set reciprocal interdependencies to find a possible way out of disaster together (Kayes, 2006). Under adverse circumstances, an organization can continue adhering to the leader's vision even when it has ceased being appropriate, thus heading for a decrease in performance, if not for a failure.

Eventually, the core message emerging from Tempest et al.'s (2007) compelling study is that 'organizations and individuals have their limits. In ignoring these, firms run the danger of disorganization and failure' (p. 1058). Running counter original theorization elaborated by Turner, the interpretation of the Himalaya incident highlights the individualism that liminality entails in the wake of adversities. By doing so, the contribution provided by Tempest et al. (2007) goes beyond the marginalization of the collective and the valorization of individual initiative that characterizes many organization studies on liminality: it posits that liminality emphasizes individualism and elicits personal responses that may jeopardize success and even survival of people and organizations. Concerning liminality in adverse situations, it has to be remembered that danger and uncertainty do pertain to liminality, as the same Turner (1969) resorted to concepts like 'death,' 'wilderness,' and 'darkness' to describe the mysterious and hazardous side of transitioning.

Along a similar way of reasoning that hones in on how organizations react against extreme events and the role of leaders in organizational crises, Teo, Lee, and Lim (2017) reported on how leaders of a Singapore hospital activated resilience in their staff to overcome an epidemic outbreak in 2003. From the first signals of the disease spread, the organization entered a liminal stage in which previous, consolidated procedures and roles had to wane since they could no longer serve to handle an impending large-scale health crisis. The relevance of leadership in managing the transition is clearly underlined and represents the gist of this study: leaders have the primary responsibility to anticipate crises and to mobilize resources to adjust to changing conditions, thus creating the premises for organizational thriving.

Leadership influence is twofold. On one hand, leaders should promote and support the development of transitional networks, i.e., reinforce extant ties based on mutual trust while facilitating the birth of new contacts through the resort to swift trust. Remarkably, from this viewpoint, the relationships that leaders should foster differ from the spontaneous, status-erasing connections that liminars set up within a communitas: they are instead relations aimed at getting access and sharing resources with other organizations to carry out a concerted action. On the other, leaders should design and implement a different structure from that operating in regular times. Teams are proposed as particularly effective organizational units. The hospital managers under exam flattened the hierarchy and simplified procedures to increase efficiency. In particular, teams composed of a seasoned and a junior doctor were formed. In ordinary shifts, it is junior doctors who perform the initial patient examination and then pass information and results on to their more experienced colleague to decide the treatment to be prescribed. On the contrary, during the epidemy, this procedure was ruled out, and an opposite way was followed: senior doctors carried out the triage, while junior colleagues were in charge of filling in prescriptions. Leaders sponsored such a significant change to protect less experienced staff from contact with potentially contagious people, preserving the hospital capacity to handle the outbreak. Eventually, combining the development of transitional networks with reliance on teams allowed the hospital to serve appropriately the population's needs in the face of an emergency.

Teo et al.'s (2017) study on liminality in teams brings to the light the anti-structure that characterizes transitions in line with the original elaboration of the liminal construct. The fading of old ways of running operations and of relating to others and its replacement with new routines and rules in fact echo the dismissal of a previous structure to embrace an anti-structure. Unlike the reflection offered by the Himalaya disaster, leaders exert here a positive influence: they ushered hospital staff to the transition that the epidemic spurred, dismantling familiar habits and replacing them with new templates. In doing so, they acted as 'absolute rulers,' marking the beginning, the development, and the end of the passage, and setting guidelines to get through it.

The double-edged influence of leadership in liminality emerges from Pina e Cunha et al.'s theoretical paper (2010) dealing with ethical issues in liminality. The role of leaders in addressing ethical concerns is traced back to three different stages: a pre-liminal stage in which the first signs of confusion and ambiguity about ethical principles can be grasped; a liminal stage in which instances of behaviors that do not adhere to ethical principles surface within a team and across teams; a post-liminal stage in which teams and the organizations they belong to justify less than ethical behaviors that have occurred in an attempt to normalize a potentially conflicting situation. The function of liminality in organizations is precisely that of opening up opportunities for revising taken-for-granted assumptions even concerning ethical issues. New interpretations and understanding are formulated, discussed, further elaborated, and eventually adopted. Liminality in teams may occur when at least two of the following aspects crash: rules (formal requirements), norms (socially validated references for action), and examples of ethical leadership (behaviors actually played out by leaders). The authors identify different patterns of collision among the above factors. In any case, leaders can trigger liminality in groups by the introduction of new rules, norms, or behaviors, but are then expected to accompany team members towards a post-liminal phase. According to Pina e Cunha, Guimarães-Costa, Rego and Clegg's (2010) study, leaders' influence is relevant, albeit not necessarily in a positive way: they can stretch the ethical boundaries of teams, introducing unfair and disturbing rules, norms, or behaviors, but it is their responsibility to see team members through the transition. The process does not always generate a more ethical context: sometimes, new rules and norms endorsed by leaders can lower the ethical standards.

The focus that reflection on teams poses on liminality recalls the articulation of roles of Turnerian tradition. A connection can be recognized between team leaders and the 'masters of ceremonies' or 'absolute rulers': individuals need guidance during passages. Studies in the organizational domain, however, point also to the difficulty to exert leadership, as emerges from the Himalayan account, when transitions are shaky and hazardous, and not predictable and recursive as those narrated in anthropology.

Finally, liminality in teams yields interesting hints that can give a twist to speculation on this topic in organizational settings. Liminality appears in fact to be particularly tricky when teams are at play. First of all, as testified by Tempest et al.'s (2007) research, if teams do not have a previous habit of working together nor any certainties to continue working together in the future, once a given objective has been achieved (e.g., Cohen and Bailey, 1997; Hackman and Wageman, 2005), the motivation to build and deepen reciprocal knowledge can be low in the face of a liminal experience (Lindkvist, 2005; Borg and Söderlund, 2015). Teammates may refrain from coalescing and hone in on individualism: mutual trust becomes therefore hard to develop. Thus, almost paradoxically, some teams of liminars, although designed with the very aim to share a common experience and fate, as was the case with Mount Everest climbers, can radically differ from communitas living transitions together. The studies on liminality in teams examined here add therefore a different perspective to the capacity of liminars to form and shape a community. In stressful circumstances in fact, unless already used to collaborating, as happened to the hospital staff handling an emergency (Teo et al., 2017), liminars may exacerbate individual agency, with possible negative consequences for the joint work the team is called to execute. If they do not invest in the comprehension of who teammates really are and what they may be able to do, liminars may be just willing to exploit others' strengths, while sidelining their weaknesses (Edward, 2011). This pattern proves to be fallible when put to the test, however, as leadership may not anymore be a guidepost to look at. Leadership is in fact controversial in team liminality, casting a shadow on the roles that accompany individuals throughout transitions. Leaders can represent a reference point in the liminal stage that prompts the creation of an anti-structure (Pina e Cunha et al., 2010), as is the case with the hospital staff handling an epidemic (Teo et al., 2017). Nevertheless, they can also represent too strong a reference that hampers the construction of a communitas and prevents team members from becoming proactive (Tempest et al., 2007). The lack of a communitas implies that team members do not develop alternative shared resources and competencies to deal with unexpected events, putting the group's success at danger.

Overall, the liminality investigated in teams is thus far deeply intertwined with emergency management: given that organizations of various types, ranging from hospitals to museums to firms, often have to face unforeseen, unsettling events (e.g., Christianson, Farkas, Sutcliffe, and Weick, 2009; Powley, 2009; Teo et al., 2017), enrichment of the theorization on liminality appears quite promising along this pathway.

The Liminal Organization

In their seminal paper on consultancy as liminality, Czarniawska and Mazza (2003) raised the appealing concept of the liminal organization. A liminal organizational refers to the 'portion' of the organization in which consultants and client's regular workers collaborate during the consulting project. Interestingly enough, consultants provide a liminal experience to others with whom they cooperate, who are temporarily suspended and detached from their ordinary tasks and patterns of interaction to work on the 'theater of images' (p. 284) that consultants offer them. Consultants' liminality is therefore contagious, affecting their client counterparts' attitudes and behaviors so much so that 'the activity of turning organizations into liminal spaces becomes a routine' (p. 286). At the same time, consultants modify their perception of being 'betwixt and between,' too, although the effect on these latter has been marginalized in the reflection on liminality based on the implicit assumption that consultants are always and invariably liminal. As the authors stressed, the presence of consultants in a company gives birth to a 'liminal organization [that] shares its legal boundaries and physical environment with a proper work organization, but it forms a virtual space, which is likely to be experienced differently by consultants and regular employees' (p. 273). An organization hosting consultants comprises a working and a liminal space: in the former, established routines are carried out and also innovation, when sought after, follows familiar processes. In the latter, the new representations conveyed by consultants are displayed, discussed, negotiated, and eventually legitimated by the working organization.

The idea of a liminal organization developing beside the working organization can be extended beyond consulting interventions to shed light on the dynamics unfolding in organizations that resort to contingent work. As has been argued above, a significant driver of the interest for liminality in organization studies lies in the diffusion of forms of contingent work and, more broadly, in the dramatic change that post-Fordist organizations have marked (Davis-Blake and Uzzi, 1993; von Hippel, Mangum, Greenberger, Heneman, and Skoglind, 1997; Barley et al., 2017). New economic orders and work processes cry out for new images, concept, and representations able to foster deeper comprehension of the dynamics at play (Barley and Kunda, 2001). The liminal organization stands out as a powerful metaphor to interpret and make sense of organizations that avail themselves of various types of contingent work, often simultaneously (George and Chattopadhyay, 2005; Barley et al., 2001). Not only can workers switch organizations based on projects (Raab and Kenis, 2009), but also relationships between organizations become mutable, with ties getting tightened or loosened throughout time, for instance, in the different stages of a new product development (Kunda et al., 2002).

The possibilities for liminal experiences to affect organizations are therefore multifaceted, and the explanatory power of liminal organizations seems as convincing and necessary as still relatively underestimated. Extending Czarniawska and Mazza's (2003) theorizing, contemporary organizations are likely to be replete with instances of liminality, as they can even simultaneously avail themselves of contingent workers with different competencies and in various units, such as project workers, consultants, and external IT specialists. At the same time, they can build networks with customers, suppliers, and other organizations, and the structure of these networks is likely variable over time (e.g. Raab and Kenis, 2009; Ellis and Ybema, 2010). A more thorough knowledge of organizations in light of multiple sources of liminality can benefit from the concept of the liminal organization acting as a creative laboratory, but requires a complex view of the interplay between liminal and working spaces. It is reasonable to conjecture that more liminal spaces may be at play simultaneously within an organization: liminal spaces can be generated, modified, and regenerated at the intersection of different sources of liminality—e.g., between consultants, IT specialists, and regular workers or between temporary workers affiliated with organizational units called to collaborate across units—with highly permeable boundaries. Based on project advancement stage or on emergent organizational necessities, contingent workers in fact can be added or dismissed, while the regular employees assigned to work with them can change as well. In parallel, the relationships with other organizations may face modifications, with some links being newly set and others left behind, some yet being reinforced, while others getting weaker over time. Consequently, in contemporary work settings liminal spaces can get more articulated and complex than originally envisaged by Czarniawska and Mazza (2003), and their interplay with working spaces continuously morphing.

If the interesting perspective of the rise of liminal organizations is bound to garner attention as work processes become increasingly fluid, it has to be thrown into sharp relief that the management of liminal organizations implies that organizations give up on traditional forms of control (Söderlund and Borg, 2017). This consideration applies to post-Fordist organizations in general (e.g., Harley, 1999; Vallas, 1999), when vertical integration is replaced by the opening of boundaries and a relaxation of hierarchical pressure. Liminal organizations developing within organizations must be handled in an adequate way, especially if the benefits of liminality are sought after, such as the generation of new ideas and a fresh outlook on resources and processes (Küpers, 2011; Bamber, Allen-Collinson, and McCormack, 2017). How creativity is really prompted in liminal organizations is yet to be comprehended. Czarniawska and Mazza (2003) posited that in liminal spaces, a repertoire of representations introduced by consultants be gauged, discussed, adjusted, and eventually adopted. Not necessarily a breakthrough emerges from a liminal space inhabited by consultants and regular workers. Rather, a shared construction of how the client company can address problems and opportunities, if not a legitimation of courses of action already identified by management, is expected (Sturdy, Handley, Clark, and Fincham, 2009; Sturdy, 2011).

In particular, liminal organizations ensuing from the confluence of multiple sources of liminality can be imbued with the positive effects of liminality that have been dealt with in Chapter 1, such as freedom and 'thinking out of the box,' but in order to attain these outcomes, an anti-structure has to come into being. The invitation not to exert traditional control in liminal organizations can be properly framed in light of this gist of liminality: the ordinary structure, with its rules, routine, and roles, needs to be abandoned or temporarily suspended in liminal spaces to make room for a new articulation of behaviors and interactions. As Clegg, Pina e Cunha, Rego, and Story (2015) argued, when uncertainty deeply characterizes organizations, the futile search for traditional forms of control turns out to be counterproductive. Since there are also downsides to liminality, which are due to negative feelings like anxiety, uncertainty, and fear, that liminars may have during a transition, through what processes the different outcomes of liminal organizations are obtained and how they are combined and valued must be left for future elucidation. The question is particularly thought-provoking and challenging in the very perspective of multiple sources of liminality simultaneously active in a single context, as claimed above.

The Aftermath of Liminality in Organizational Settings

There are of course consequences related to liminal processes unfolding in organizational contexts. Negative effects like anxiety and uncertainty related to the future evolution, as well as positive outcomes like being creative and thinking without constraints, may apply to liminal phenomena in organizational settings as to any liminal experiences in general. Learning is the kernel of liminality that has been thrown into sharp relief when work processes are concerned, though. Being exposed to different settings in which to enjoy variable sets of relationships, project workers can receive stimuli to view resources and processes from different perspectives and come up with new ideas about how to rearrange them (Borg and Söderlund, 2013, 2015). A learning driver undergirds, in many cases, the very decision to become independent knowledge workers, able to switch organizations and therefore to gain access to heterogeneous contexts, becoming 'gurus' in the market (Barley and Kunda, 2004). Individuals who opt for a career as project workers and become liminars, according to the prevalent view in the organizational studies that have been taken into account, are attracted by the very opportunity for continuous learning that changing workplace urges (Garsten, 1999).

The learning process that can be gleaned from liminal experiences remains controversial, however. Individuals can increase their specialized competencies—e.g., IT professional or web designer—when moving from project to project, since they enjoy the chance of applying competencies to heterogeneous setting, enriching their body of knowledge (Tempest and Starkey, 2004). Working for different companies or, within the same company, for different units, enables professionals to build a 'portfolio of experiences' that increases their attractiveness in the market (Tempest and Starkey, 2004).

What is claimed to be missing in liminal experiences is the possibility to develop an understanding of organizational processes. Client companies in fact carefully define in what activities contingent workers can participate and with what informants they can interact: by doing so, management aim at preserving the companies' core competencies from potential 'leakages' ensuing from temporary workers moving from firm to firm (Inkson, Heising, and Rousseau, 2001; Borg and Söderlund, 2015). Contingent workers therefore face a likely paradox: they enhance their professional skills, while diminishing their ability to interpret and intervene upon organizational processes. The liminality attributed to the various types of contingent work, in this perspective, may allow individuals to develop their expertise further, but widens the gap between them and their client organizations, thus reducing the chances to be someday, if wished, incorporated as regular employees (Borg and Söderlund, 2015). The distance from house learning activities and company information intentionally designed by client companies' management may fragilize individuals in the long term, almost tying them to a future as independent workers (Garsten, 1999). Winkler and Mahmood (2015) went to the point to question the positive effect that mobility across organizations can actually bear on individual learning: they underlined the lack of a virtuous intertwining between professional knowledge and organizational knowledge that contingent workers suffer from and that can end up penalizing them. Relatedly, Tempest and Starkey (2004) argued that mobile workers may not fully benefit from their 'passages' in client organizations, for instance, by taking time to reflect on the projects completed before undertaking new assignments as they feel the constant pressure to find contracts and not to remain inactive.

A complex framework is offered by the impact of the resort to contingent work on organizations as well. By availing themselves of competencies on demand, client companies can forge relationships with more talent than that internally available, and stretch and squeeze the pool of resources they can rely on upon necessity (Tempest and Starkey, 2004). Likewise, client companies can capitalize on the network that mobile workers are endowed with and offer. Contingent workers can in fact provide access to different firms, institutions, and freelancers that they have previously known and interacted with. In this sense, workers who juggle arrangements with various organizations can be seen as 'bees,' 'serially pollinating organizations with learning' (Inkson et al., 2001, p. 276). Similarly to what was stressed above about the consequences of liminality on individual learning, contingent work is not devoid of intricacies for organizations, however. Retaining competencies over time can become challenging for firms that employ intensively contingent workers, since a short-term orientation, also critically referred to as 'short-termism,' can lessen managerial investments in actions aimed at fostering organizational members' organizational commitment and identification (Söderlund and Borg, 2018). In a related vein, Wagner et al. (2012) showed how a project like the design of an enterprise system can generate a liminal experience for the project team members, who operate in a dedicated space with reduced contacts with colleagues not involved in the project. Although the project phases can be accomplished effectively, the success of its subsequent implementation can be jeopardized by the capability of team members to effectively share the project-related knowledge with a wider audience of organizational members. In the case recounted by Wagner and coauthors (2012), liminal experiences are not sufficient to create learning, but the premises for learning to extend beyond liminal spaces and affect the organization as a whole must be carefully designed. To this regard, the enterprise system project under study called for an intensive negotiation effort, based upon a conciliatory attitude, between those who had undertaken it firsthand and its users to settle divergent perspectives.

It is noteworthy that, as much debated as the interplay between liminality and learning might still be, evidence from liminality in the organizational settings examined brings to the fore the relationship between learning and identity work (Söderlund and Borg, 2018). This link has been fleshed out from several perspectives. When consultancy is at stake, remarkably, not only does it convey learning opportunities to both the client company and the consulting team (Sturdy et al., 2009; Sturdy, 2011), but even reflexivity on the client company identity is spurred. From the more straightforward revision of some operating processes or legitimation of decisions to the more demanding redesign of organizational structure and elaboration of a new strategy, firms that avail themselves of consulting projects not only enjoy the opportunity to understand what resources and competencies they already detain and what else need to be accessed, but also start questioning who they are as an organization and who they may become following the change implementation (Goodman, 1978; Clegg et al., 2004). As Clegg et al. (2004, p. 41) argued about the profound effect that consulting projects can have on the core features of an organization and the identity work that they can prompt, 'all processes of organizational transformation are processes that are not entirely controllable and manageable because they imply the deconstruction, deterritorialization and reversing of existing practices and images that frame an organization's actual possibilities.'

Identity work has been associated with learning in career transitions interpreted as liminal experiences (Ibarra, 1999; Ibarra and Barbulescu, 2010), too. Moving towards a new role or, even more, towards a new profession requires that new skills and competencies be acquired as well a new identity be developed and negotiated. Concerning the passage from executive to higher hierarchical position, Ibarra, Snook, and Ramo (2010) underlined the identity work that people have to engage in to develop a new sense of self as leaders, not just as senior managers. The main assumption here is that identity work related to career advancements leads to a dramatic variation in individuals' thoughts, feelings, and behaviors to fit in the new tasks and obligations. Along this way of reasoning, Tansley and Tietze (2013) connected identity work to talent management to adapt to new roles. Their study adopted a lens particularly tailored to liminality in which handling talent growth necessitates a series of rites of passage, such as participation in 'stretch projects,' undertaking professional exams, and involvement in exchanges between talent peers, managers, and mentors. Separation rites serve to mark the detachment of individuals from a former role and 'locate 'talent' in temporary, ambiguous situations where they have yet to master the rules of engagement for subsequent stages and achieve 'full membership' of the most senior group' (Tansley and Tietze, 2013, p. 1810). In the 'gray areas' that separation rites unlock, identity work and development of an understanding of what activities and interactions the new role will entail intermingle and pave the way for the 'realignment from talented graduate, to young professional, to senior consultant to leader' (p. 1811) that incorporation rites intend to celebrate.

In addition, Ryan (2019) claimed that knowledge sharing was related to identity work among boundary spanners in a liminal experience. Organizational learning is partly driven by the identity work of boundary spanners, who, positioning themselves across organizations, are deemed to be liminal. In the case of a financial director and a festival manager collaborating to set up an art event (Ryan, 2019), by alternatively acting as guide and ally to each other and by facing together the transition that the joint initiative represents, a new 'us' was formed. Incremental learning was intertwined with this emergent social identity. The festival director in fact attended financial workshops held at the partner's company and organized an audit in his own firm. As a consequence, he was recognized by his organization's members as a manager with a financial expertise, changing his self-view. Similarly, the financial manager learned how to integrate arts and engineering/business, for instance, by providing timely responses to the last-minute requests that often arise when handling artistic initiatives. Learning was developed and shared in the 'safe space' that the two managers settled as a holding environment for their liminal experience and connected identity work (Ellis and Ybema, 2010; Petriglieri et al., 2019). While a common identity was constructed, the self-concept was modified: when reincorporated into their employing companies after running the art festival, the art director had integrated an identity as financial expert, while the financial manager had reinforced his previous artistic vein and personal identity as film fan. Both professionals ended their shared liminal experience with a changed view of self and changed expertise that they could bring back to their respective organizations.

Finally, if the issue of whether and how liminal experiences urge individual and/or organizational learning remains controversial, the link between learning and identity work comes out in a convincing way from empirical and theoretical reflection in organizational contexts. In this field, liminality is a vital 'monster of doubt' through which perspectives are transformed and individuals experiment ideologies and identities that could not be envisioned in regular life and work conditions (Hawkins and Edwards, 2015). The process that links knowledge and identity work is fascinating and represents an authentically original view on liminality that its framing in organizational settings offers to the wider, cross-field debate on this topic (Table 2.2).

Table 2.2 Elaboration of the core features of organizational liminal experiences

Main features	Emergent issues in organization studies	Contributions
Timelessness and spacelessness	Interpreting some habitual spaces as liminal Inhabiting multiple spaces without feeling to belong to any of them Being located in a separate space	Di Domenico et al. (2014); Shortt (2015); Daniel and Ellis-Chadwick (2016); Caza et al. (2017); Vesala and Tuomivaara (2018); Söderlund and Borg (2018)
Rites, ceremonies, and symbols	Rhythms and cycles telling activity from activity, individual activities from collective activities, working life from personal life, becoming blurred	Czarniawska and Mazza (2003); Sturdy et al. (2006, 2009); Czarniawska and Mazza (2012)
Anti-structure	Generating alternative routines, rules, and norms Possible overlapping with established social order and structure	Sturdy et al. (2006, 2009); Ibarra and Obodaru (2016)
Communitas	'Threshold people' Lack of a sense of togetherness Difficulty to tie bonds among liminars Organizational effort rather than liminars' initiatives to set up relationships among liminars	Garsten (1999); Küpers (2011); Garcia-Lorenzo et al. (2018)
Individual agency	Individual practices to secure a work identity Individual practices to handle job assignments Repertoires to manage relationships along the value chain Synchronizing and harmonizing multiple work roles 'Mental mobility' to handle different spaces	Ellis and Ybema (2010); Borg and Söderlund, (2015); Swan et al. (2016); Caza et al. (2017); Petriglieri et al. (2019)

Main features	Emergent issues in organization studies	Contributions
Identity work	Inherently dynamic and ambiguous process. Strongly interrelated with learning	Thurlow and Helms Mills (2009); Ellis and Ybema (2010); Ibarra et al. (2010); Tansley and Tietze (2013); Hawkins and Edwards (2015); Ryan (2019)
Aftermaths	Stress and frustration related to future work perspectives. Creativity targeting new business ventures and work process innovations. Controversial effect on individual and organizational learning	Inkson et al. (2001); Clegg et al. (2004); Söderlund (2004); Tempest and Starkey (2004); Borg and Söderlund (2013, 2015); Winkler and Mahmood (2015); Schulz et al. (2016); Demetry, 2017; Vesala and Tuomivaara (2018)

Conclusion

Liminality in organization studies is deeply nested within contemporary society evolution. The growing interest and application of this lens to make sense of phenomena are in fact embedded in the changes that work processes have undergone over the past decades. In particular, it is to the diffusion of various forms of contingent work, e.g., project work or temporary assignments, that the attention towards this construct can be attributed (e.g., Garsten, 1999; Borg and Söderlund, 2013, 2015). At the same time, career pathways have been changing, leading to the pursuit of multiple careers in parallel, such as hybrid entrepreneurship, due to an economic driver or to the search for an authenticity of the self (e.g., Alboher, 2007; Caza et al., 2017). The mutable nature of work processes has provided impetus to liminality in organizations expanding on a stream of studies that had previously focused on consultancy as a privileged unit of analysis (e.g., Czarniawska and Mazza, 2003; Sturdy et al., 2006).

In embracing liminality to make sense of changes in work processes, the core features undergirding this construct have assumed different meanings and nuances compared to Turner's reflection. Some of the elements examined in Chapter 1 have been marginalized, while others have been given prominence or have even garnered recognition just in organizational settings. An overview of the relevant interpretations is provided in Table 2.2. Rites, ceremonies, and symbols are parsed out especially in studies on consultancy: they are fluid and recursive, signaling the beginning, the development, and end of projects and the related variable roles taken on by consultants and client company's members throughout the different stages (e.g., Czarniawska and Mazza, 2003; Sturdy et al., 2006). But for a few notable exceptions, though, rites are not considered to be a salient aspect of liminal experience in organizations, as rituals appear to fit into institutionalized societies rather than contemporary, more fluctuating contexts (Ibarra and Obodaru, 2016). The scant attention devoted to rites in organization studies on liminality is all the more striking given the relevance that they assume in role transitions (Ashforth, Kreiner, and Fugate, 2000), career transitions (Mayrhofer and Iellatchitch, 2005), and socialization to professions and organizations (Hallier and James, 1999).

Concerning spacelessness, it can be traced back to three different types in the field under study that all mark a separation from how places are usually inhabited as well as from people who are not in transition. First, some places, which are part of regular work or life spaces, prompt and encompass a liminal experience when used differently, e.g., to take a break from tight scheduling and enjoy some relaxation (e.g., Shortt, 2015). A second liminal use of spaces can be traced back to the dwelling in more places, while feeling to fully belong to none of them and, at the same time, to all of them, as is the case with hybrid entrepreneurship or multiple careers unfolding in different locations (e.g., Daniel and Ellis-Chadwick, 2016; Caza et al., 2017). A third way lies in being temporarily secluded in a separate and alien location (e.g., Wagner et al., 2012; Vesala and Tuomivaara, 2018).

Timelessness revamps the cyclical connotation of liminality in traditional societies: the different perception of time flow compared to how it used to be and to the perception of people who are not involved in a liminal experience is due to the fading of regularity and to the blurring of the boundaries between distinct work activities, between working and personal life, and between individual and collective activities (e.g., Vesala and Tuomivaara, 2018). In other words, time pace marks a significant contrast between liminars and non-liminars (Söderlund and Borg, 2018).

As regards anti-structure, it remains quite overshadowed in reflection about liminal experiences in organizations: little or nothing seems to be predefined in current transition. Roles, norms, and new routines have to be constructed and negotiated throughout the transition itself, without any previous, enduring arrangements to look at (e.g., Ibarra and Obodaru, 2016; Ryan, 2019). Remarkably, when an alternative structure arises from a liminal experience, it tends to coexist, and sometimes to overlap or even interfere, with established order, not to replace or erase it (e.g., Sturdy et al., 2006, 2009).

The feature of liminality that is more surprisingly sidelined in organization studies, however, is the social dimension of liminality, well represented by the communitas that is formed among individuals facing a common transition. The sense of 'togetherness' that is felt by members of a tribe preparing for adulthood (e.g., Turner, 1974b) or by individuals who go through a similar disease (e.g., Brown, Huszar, and Chapman, 2017) is missing in the field under study. With few relevant exceptions, such as the ties established among unemployed people (Daskalaki and Simosi, 2018) or among nascent entrepreneurs (Garcia-Lorenzo et al., 2018)), it is rather individual agency that comes up as typical of liminal experiences in organizations. Liminars in fact build and apply their own practices to cope with the suspension that they experiment with: such practices can be behavioral like ways to handle job assignments or to manage connections with a variety of organizations (Ellis and Ybema, 2010; Borg and Söderlund, 2015), as well as cognitive, as is the case with harmonizing multiple careers' requirements or the 'mental mobility' expected of individuals who switch organizations on a project basis (Borg and Söderlund, 2015; Caza et al., 2017). Liminality experiences in the organizational realm is devoid of a collective impetus and replete with instances of individual responses. This scenario stands in marked contrast to the need for bonding and sharing among peers depicted not only in anthropology, as recalled above, but also in other fields like medicine and sociology, as reported in Chapter 1. If the individual dimension throws new light on the dynamics of liminality unfolding in and across organizations, it is not exclusive of this domain, as will be argued in the next chapter.

The perspective on liminality linked to organizational phenomena moves away from the original conceptualization even in terms of identity work. Imagining, testing, and revising identity is brought to the fore in this field and is strongly intertwined with a learning process (e.g., Tansley and Tietze, 2013; Hawkins and Edwards, 2015). Individuals are engaged in learning new tasks, rules, and patterns of interaction as they try to come to terms with who they are and who they might become, although this essentially dynamic process is imbued with some ambiguity. Ambiguity can be grasped in the difficulty to comprehend whether the effects of the learning opportunities triggered in liminal situations are beneficial for individuals who embark upon transitions and/or for the organizations to which they are connected, in the end. The issue still remains open and controversial, with as many contributions testifying to a positive influence as those pointing to potential drawbacks (e.g., Tempest and Starkey, 2004; Winkler and Mahmood, 2015). It is worth underlining, however, that in the very link between identity work and learning and in the enhancement of individual agency seem to reside the most valuable and original insights on liminality provided by organizational reflection.

It has also to be stressed that a striking point of liminality in the organizational domain is that it is an attribute of a given state or role rather than a perception of suspension between a 'here' and 'there'. Although the different studies on this topic that are analyzed in this chapter have fleshed out various aspects of liminal experiences like individual proactivity or the feelings of uncertainty and stress, they share a similar assumption: certain situations, such as being a consultant, a nascent entrepreneur, or the member of an adventure team trying to climb up Mount Everest, unequivocally evoke a liminal experience. This framing of liminality represents an oversimplification of the plethora of interpretations, feelings, and perceptions that different individuals may instead develop in what is treated as one and the same situation.

An exception to this view resides in research that delves into liminality sparked by significant jolts like an accident, a job loss, or the participation in an event (O'Loughlin et al., 2017; Jahn et al., 2018). In these occasions, individuals quit a previous situation to enter a new, uncertain, and often undesired 'gray area,' being unsecure or unaware of what may lie ahead for them. Söderlund and Borg (2018) theorized about the three typologies of liminality that are tackled by organizational literature, i.e., process, position, and state. The process typology can be properly applied to studies on liminality as triggered by jolts. Under these circumstances in fact, liminal experiences are argued to unfold through the three phases indicated in Chapter 1—separation, liminality, and incorporation—that lead from a previous state or role to a subsequent one. Studies that hinge on the process perspective embrace van Gennep and Turner's original approach and focus on 'individuals' transitioning between different states, situations and professional identities' (Söderlund and Borg, 2018, pp. 5–6).

Conversely, the analysis of the contributions to liminality that has been performed in this chapter points to the prominence of a vision centered upon states and roles as indicators of liminality, and leaves us with a core question: Do really all individuals in a given state or role feel liminal? Put differently, do consultants, temporary workers, or managers of interorganizational networks perceive and acknowledge their being 'betwixt and between' in one and the same way? Are they necessarily liminal personae in transition from a familiar past situation to an impending one due to their state or position? The following chapters will address this core question by resorting to the latest advancements in research in various fields, beyond the organizational realm that has been the object of this chapter, which have been significantly touched and intrigued by liminality, as well, and can inform a richer understanding of this construct.

3 Emergent Perspectives on Liminality

Introduction

Research on liminality has been burgeoning not only in organization studies, but also in other fields. The surge of interest for liminality has, on one hand, enriched our understanding of this concept by adding nuances to some of its core elements or proposing new elements to frame it, but on the other has weakened it, blurring the distinction between liminality and other concepts already familiar to the organizational behavior literature. The temporal dimension of liminality has been the focus of major revision: this chapter will show that, moving away from the original interpretation as a temporary stage of the transition from a previously known situation to a future one, evidence on liminality has advanced the view that it may become prolonged over time, even permanent, or that it may be so often repeated throughout the working and personal life to make any incorporation ephemeral. A different vision of time is also related to the possibility of the liminal experience to evolve while it is lived, changing its content and meaning. In addition, different forms of liminality can be faced simultaneously by an individual within the same domain, be it the working or personal life, or across domains. The complex time dynamics surfacing from studies that adopt this construct as an interpretive lens provide stimuli to mostly speculate, so far, that there may be different degrees of the liminality perceived even in allegedly similar situations, such as being a temporary worker, a migrant, or a patient in remission. Finally, from yet a different stance, research on liminality in contemporary society has reinforced the evidence of the construction of practices that at an individual, group, or organizational level lay the foundation for creating a viable alternative to the social order that 'being betwixt and between' leaves behind.

Liminality as a Protracted Experience

The word able to better grasp and synthesize the meaning of liminality conceived of in anthropology is transition. Liminality, as described in Chapter 1, represents in fact the central phase of a passage from a previous state or role to something different, often partially or thoroughly unknown when the transition begins. As with any passages, liminality is therefore intended to come to an end at a certain time. The limited duration of liminal experiences has been frequently questioned, though. The same Victor Turner at various points envisaged the possibility for liminality to become permanent. He referred to groups like the Franciscans and the Hippies, for whom personal relationships take over social obligations, time flows according to idiosyncratic rhythms, and spaces are secluded, as permanently liminal in his 1969 writing. He later extended this consideration to contemporary societies by acknowledging the likelihood of 'a style of life that is permanently contained within liminality [...] Instead of the liminal being a passage, it seemed to be coming to be regarded as a state' (1974b, p. 261). Turner (1982) also raised the issue of long-term liminality when addressing the liminoid, assigning this perspective to the situation of writers and rock stars, who have intermittent and short-lived appointments throughout their working life and therefore live continuously in transition.

Many studies in heterogeneous fields have gleaned from the suggestion that liminality may be an enduring experience. The assumption that underlies liminality ceasing to be a passage is that contemporary societies be dramatically different from the traditional societies that inspired theorizing on liminality, and a gist of the current transformation is that liminality may not be just a transient experience (Horvath, Thomassen, and Wydra, 2015). The less institutionalized and normative societies become, the more liminality turns into an 'institutionalized and ongoing phenomenon' (Söderlund and Borg, 2018, p. 889) that can be protracted indefinitely. It is at a higher level therefore that liminality is legitimized as a stretched phenomenon: Szakolczai (2000) got to the point to diagnose modernity as the realm of permanent liminality. On a related note, building upon evidence on changes in labor processes, the shift to long-term liminality as a characteristic of epochs, before even that of individuals and groups, has been avowed by various scholars (Thomassen, 2009, 2014; Jordhus-Lier, Underthun, and Zampoukos, 2017; Underthun and Jordhus-Lier, 2018).

Ibarra and Obodaru (2016, p. 50) effectively expressed the interpretation of liminality length as an 'open-ended, extended time period.' The difference between time-bounded transitions and longer, even permanent liminality has been clearly defined by Ybema et al. (2011) as a sense of unending 'betweenness,' and refined further by Bamber, Allen-Collinson, and McCormack (2017, p. 1516), as follows: '[while] transitional liminality generates a sense of being *not-X-anymore-and-not-Y-yet*, permanent liminality creates a more permanent sense of being *neither-X-nor-Y* or *both-X-and-Y*' [italics in the original]. Such view is rooted in the observation that many instances of liminality reported in the literature do not highlight a starting nor an ending point, but rather the persistence of a same situation over time.

Taking move from organization studies, most work arrangements analyzed in the previous chapter testify to the intention not to choose—or maybe the impossibility to attain—a stable way of working, with a single, enduring affiliation to an employing organization (e.g., Garsten, 1999; Barley and Kunda, 2004). Contingent work in fact is often due to last over time through the reiteration of contracts with diverse client companies, and does not represent a stimulating, but maybe unsettling interstice between two permanent full-time jobs (Söderlund and Borg, 2018).

Lasting liminality has been coupled with the notion of 'limbo' as suitable to grasp the existential experience of liminality under given circumstances (Cohn, 2001; Czarniawska and Mazza, 2003; Pace and Pallinster-Wilkins, 2018; Richter, 2018). Limbo stems from the Latin word *limbus*, which means edge or border. Although it may sound close to the *limen* that gives birth to liminality, its difference can be comprehended by recalling how it is portrayed by Dante Alighieri (2017) in the *Divine Comedy* following the Catholic religion dogma: dwellers in the limbo are condemned to remain suspended and to endlessly long for deliverance, although they have committed no specific sin. Limbo well captures the recorded evolution of liminality into a long-term experience that entails no desired or possible way out.

Bamber et al. (2017) expanded on speculation on limbo in liminal experiences by theorizing specifically about occupational limbo. Their study unraveled that individuals who had teaching-only positions in British universities felt that they would likely continue having this role without any concrete opportunities to turn into all-round academics called to do also research. Belief of the unlikelihood to reach a wanted state generates unpleasant and disruptive feelings that can be synthesized as 'locked-in-ness.' Drawing on this evidence, the authors claimed that occupational limbo can be traced back to being '*always-this-and-never-that*, where *this* is less desirable than *that*' (p. 1514; italics in the original). In the higher education settings under exam, *this* is the scarcely appealing teaching-only position, whereas *that* is the more attractive academic position. Unlike permanent liminality, limbo generates 'trapped souls' that do not head for a threshold to be crossed: their unease and frustration can be overcome either by a significant change, such as a major career move or a modification of the institutional framework in which they are embedded, or by an impressive individual reaction within the given framework.

The persistence of liminality is fraught with potential drawbacks. The uncertainty linked to a prolonged suspension can negatively affect personal life since it exacerbates the conflict between the often divergent requirements and logics of work and private life (Johnsen and Sørensen, 2015). In the case of consultants as permanently liminal actors analyzed by these authors, their being 'all-nighters' in the face of impending deadlines blurs any distinction between work and life for years, thus impairing the attainment of a work-life balance. The symbolic stress associated with the perpetual danger (Turner, 1967) that a long-term liminality impels turns consultancy into a 'lifestyle' in which work and personal life get intermingled in a growingly puzzling way. The result of a lasting liminality may also be a 'body in pain,' not just a mind in anguish (Johnsen and Sørensen, 2015, p. 329).

A similar pattern can be found in temporary workers who stick to this type of employment in the long run. Frequent changes of client companies lead individuals to shape their lives according to these latter's location, undergoing geographical displacements and facing a distance from home that turn out to be particularly demanding for workers who have a partner or a family, putting a strain on their affective relationships (Winkler and Mahmood, 2015).

Creativity, which is a major point of strength of liminal experiences, may be also threatened or at least weakened by permanent liminality. The promising capability to subvert the status quo and to imagine brand new pathways is diminished when suspension extends so long that it becomes ordinary in itself. A prolonged suspension turns then into a consolidated state that limits the likelihood to identify and implement significant changes. As a consequence, only incremental changes are expectable when liminality ends up being a real transition to become a stable way of working (Ryan, 2019; Söderlund and Borg, 2018).

The extension of liminality beyond a time-bound experience is testified in heterogeneous fields. Bicultural people live permanently under the influence of different, sometimes conflicting cultures, constantly questioning and trying to conciliate their affiliations, while feeling suspended between two or even more worlds (Nguyen and Benet-Martínez, 2013). Sociology of migration and of health has conveyed meaningful accounts of permanent liminality. In her ethnographic account of the life of Mali migrants stuck in Algerian and Moroccan camps on their way to Europe, Richter (2016) narrated the limbo that they experienced as they had left behind their country and secured connections, but were unable to make the final leap to Europe, which was their aspired final destination. Permanence in Maghreb countries would last months, years, or even forever, as individuals felt the impossibility to go back home, which would be interpreted as a total failure, but also to proceed in their travel, thus nourishing the sensation to be stuck in a limbo: 'The Malian migrants find themselves in a pinch. They are literally at the edge of Europe, which they can see in the distance from where they are, but are not sure they will make it there.' (Richter, 2016, p. 77).

Albeit with completely different premises, evidence from patients with chronical diseases, an enduring disability, or in recovery from cancer tells similar stories of indeterminateness and suspension, hope and disillusion, and ambiguous belongingness to the worlds of the sick and of the healthy people due to their lasting condition. Individuals suffering from myalgic encephalomyelitis, chronic fatigue syndrome, or high cholesterol, for instance, feel permanently liminal, as they are feeling neither too bad nor totally well and they do not foresee any future closure to their current way of living (Hoel Felde, 2011; Brown, Huszar, and Chapman, 2017). Studies on disability have shown similar patterns: people with special needs perceive to be 'between the sick role and normality, between wrong bodies and right bodies' (Phillips, 1990, p. 851). To this regard, Moran (2013) noted that the sense of not being able to emerge from the state of in-betweenness is heightened by the barriers that society create, through the setup of elevated standards, to prevent a social reincorporation and thus crystallize a destabilizing difference. Disabled persons can therefore come to see themselves, and to be seen by others, as permanently placed outside the mainstream and no longer in transition towards any new state, but forever entrapped in a painful fuzziness (Reid-Cunningham, 2009; Adorno, 2015; Cronin, Ryrie, Huntley, and Hayton, 2018).

On a related note, several studies have tapped into cancer as a disease potentially leading to long-term liminality. Little, Jordens, Paul, Montgomery, and Philipson (1998) described the journey towards various forms of liminality that people affected by this sickness embark upon. Upon the diagnosis of their illness, individuals experiment with a first type of liminality ensuing from the awareness of their modified state and the necessity to undergo a period of treatments and therapies. Once the 'acute' liminal experience ends because treatments are over and recovery is officially acknowledged, they enter a so-called 'chronic' liminality in which they continue feeling 'betwixt and between' life and death, and health and illness, and inhabit a long-term 'gray area' paced by medical checkups and underscored by body changes. The perception of being permanently liminal is, in these cases, reinforced if relapses occur, triggering the whole cycle again and pushing liminality further into a fixed condition (Thompson, 2007; Blows, Bird, Seymour, and Cox, 2012).

The idea that liminality may become long-term, even everlasting, and not just a temporary experience bound to lead individuals towards a new, likely more appealing way of being, has gained momentum in a variety of fields and has availed itself of a range of perspectives. It is therefore undeniable that enduringness represents a view on liminal experiences in contemporary societies that has to be taken into account, although, as will be discussed in the following chapter, it risks blurring and disempowering the construct of liminality.

Liminality as a Repeated (and Repeatable) Experience

Not only the duration of liminal experiences has been called into question by recent research on this theme, but also the possibility to reiterate liminal experiences throughout the working and/or personal life has been garnering attention. Along the timeline of an individual's life, multiple transitions can be passed through and cumulate. According to this stance, liminality may consist of a series of short, but repeated periods of passage. Unlike the major transitions that can accompany human life in anthropology, such as the passage from adolescence to adulthood, from singlehood to a married status, or from ordinary member to chief of a tribe, people can sort temporarily out of their ordinary trajectories to engage in novel courses of action, inhabit different spaces, experiment with unusual time rhythms, be exposed to different rules, routines, and social interactions, and receive stimuli for identity work. These movements in and out of situational factors that continue, none-theless, being prominent take the shape of repeated liminal experiences. Liminality becomes then intermittent, be it at a regular or irregular pace.

Recurrent liminality was attributed to teaching activities that remove children from everyday activities (Atkinson and Robson, 2012). Creative arts-based interventions occur regularly, e.g., on a weekly basis, but have the potential to represent an experience of suspension. Based on this study, primary school children are involved in a different space from their classroom, with a different time management, different classmates, a different teacher, to perform different activities from those characterizing usual learning patterns in the classroom. All this difference bears resemblance to a liminal experience, and its outcome is line with liminal expectations; temporarily detached from ordinary habits and routines, children free up their imagination, release the performance-related anxiety, and attain social and emotional well-being. Allowing 'short but repeated periods of separation' (Atkinson and Robson, 2012, p. 1350) adds a contemporary nuance to the disruption of existing structures of thought and feelings undergirding Turner's (1977, p. 68) claim on the essence of liminality:

> For me the essence of liminality is to be found in its release from normal constraints, making possible the deconstruction of the "uninteresting" constructions of common sense, the "meaningfulness of ordinary life."

Unlike original theorization of liminality, though, reiterative liminality is endowed with permeable barriers. Ordinary life surfaces in liminal spaces and times, and has to be managed. For instance, children brought to creative arts sessions their tensions and fears arising from family dynamics and from other school activities and priorities that could be disruptive and impair the effectiveness of alternative activities like drawing and dancing. As Atkinson and Robson (2012, p. 1353) stated, 'Contemporary settings of liminality, with their flexible temporalities are vulnerable to intrusions from the wider context in ways that Turner's settings of total and protracted withdrawal were not.' Remarkably, though, intrusions can become beneficial over time, since their occurrence prevents the liminal experience from turning into a 'sanctuary,' i.e., a secluded portion of time and space whose effects would not be integrated into participants' everyday world.

Frequently exiting and reentering ordinary life through travels has been interpreted in light of reiterative liminality, too. Tourists are liminal in that they quit, albeit temporarily, their homes, work, and patterns of interactions to navigate new realms and expose themselves to unknown stimuli, sometimes even to transgressions that would not be approached elsewhere (Pritchard and Morgan, 2006; Huang, Xiao, and Wang, 2018). Not only the various destinations of a trip, with their articulated social representations, constitute a break from a familiar order and interiorized routines, but also physical locations that act as intermediate spaces enabling travels, such as hotels and airports, are liminal experiences per se (Pritchard and Morgan, 2006). Consequently, the tourism field offers a view on liminality similar to 'Chinese boxes' in which multiple experiences are layered and intertwined with each other even within what may be identified as a single trip. Every change of location implies a new transition and therefore a limited liminal experience within a broader one. This liminality arrangement is particularly embodied in the life choices of the so-called 'lifestyle travelers,' 'permanent tourists,' or 'lifelong wanderers' who choose to travel for a long period of time, moving from place to place and settling down for only short periods in each site (Noy and Cohen, 2005; Sharpley and Sundaram, 2005; Cohen, 2011). Traveling on a long run blurs the distinction between orderliness and passage, as the protracted detachment that being far away, frequently switching locations, engenders leaves individuals wondering where they really belong to and what they can reasonably call home (and regularity).

Bui, Wilkins, and Lee (2014) offered an interesting insight on the feelings and emotions of young Asian backpackers undertaking months-long trips. Given the collectivism of Asian societies, individual backpacking provides a fertile setting to investigate liminal experiences, as the engagement in solitary initiatives eluding taken-for-granted rules and norms of public life adds further suspension and indeterminacy to the already liminal traveling. Taking distance from daily routines and encountering new contexts is at the same time stimulating and destabilizing, as the desire to explore alternative ways of living is coupled with intense homesickness and nostalgia. While feeling free from the constraints imposed upon by familiar relationships is empowering, young travelers at the same time revamp their affective attachment to the network they belong to at home and reinforce their personal identity. As Bui et al. (2014, p. 132) reported, 'The liminal experience of the Asian backpackers is a negotiation between the motivation to escape from home and the sense of connection to home.'

Repeated liminality can also be a daily experience in which boundaries are crossed multiple times. This is the case of commuting as recounted by Wilhoit's (2017) study. Commuting from home to work and back becomes in the actors' narrative a 'sacred time' that is neither home nor workplace, and neither family time nor work time. Traveling back and forth is an interstice that resonates with liminality in Turner's interpretation as individuals are aware of what they leave behind (work or home) and what lies ahead (home or work), while having to comply with the rules and duties of none of these spheres. Conversely, commuters can fill their liminal situation with daydreaming, cultivating their passions like reading or writing, or just enjoying alone time devoid of social obligations (Nippert-Eng, 1996, 2008). From this perspective, commuting is seen as a break from the social order of work and personal life that is embraced and released on a regular basis, thus becoming, quite counterintuitively, a routine liminality.

Moran (2013) offered evidence of recurrent liminality in an extreme case, that of Russian prisons' visiting suites, which could reinforce theorizing about this emergent feature. Visiting suites are spaces within jail precincts where prisoners are allowed to spend some time—usually a few days—with their families. These places are set up like hostels, albeit of a basic kind, that can be rented, upon prison management permission, to recreate a domestic setting where objects can be brought from home and typical familiar activities like cooking, watching TV, and preparing meals can be enacted. Visiting suites can be considered as liminal spaces since they are temporarily inhabited by prisoners and their families, giving birth to a blended and ambiguous experience (Comfort, 2003). On the relatives' side in fact, a 'secondary prisonization' has been evoked, as they have to give up on some of their freedom, while testing an 'inside' experience. At the same time, prisoners get access to an 'outside' taste, as they interact with people and objects that belong to the external world. When residing in the suits, inmates are freed from the 'deprivation of autonomy' and the 'deprivation of goods and services' that pertain to permanence in jail. Interestingly, the entry into a liminal space is underlined by rites, such as surrendering the cell phones and undergoing strict security checks.

Prisoners' life can comprise multiple liminal experiences in the visiting suites throughout their detention, each of which is bound to end and bring individuals back to their previous state. Consequently, 'liminal spaces can constitute a frustratingly repetitive, static or equilibrating form of transformation which is cumulative rather than immediate' (Moran, 2013, p. 339). Liminality can be not a linear transformation towards a new state or role, as shown by Turner, but a recursive elusion from, and reintegration into, a same state or role. Reiterated liminal experiences therefore are neither phases in transitions from a past to a future situation nor a limbo: they function like a 'rubber band' intermittently moving individuals back and forth without significantly modifying their position.

Repeated liminality instances or similarities can be identified also in organizational contexts. The experience of journalists, graphic designers, engineers, and other professionals in an alternative workplace (an archipelago) to find inspiration for changes in their daily work routines paves the way for further subsequent interruptions of the status quo to seek sources of creativity (Vesala and Tuomivaara, 2018). Liminality can therefore be reiterated over time, with the expectation that, once reintegrated into their previous life, individuals carry with them the potential to modify their reality.

A nuanced interpretation of repeated liminality able to make a distinction between temporary and permanent experiences is yielded by Ryan (2019) and by Jahn, Cornwell, Drengner, and Gaus (2018) in their elaborations of temporary incorporation. In narrating the organization of an arts festival as an opportunity to spawn liminality, Ryan (2019) claimed that even when a thoroughly liminal experience according to the Turner's view is accomplished with a reincorporation—in the case studied, the managers under exam regained their role in their employing organizations, reincorporation is nevertheless to be deemed temporary, as 'the subject and the context continue to change' (p. 350). The potential for change that individuals who have undergone a liminal experience introduce into the settings to which they are affiliated opens up the way for additional liminal experiences and, remarkably, for incremental learning linked to liminality. From this perspective, liminality generates temporary incorporation and is generated by temporary incorporation, as liminality imbues contexts with the seeds of change. Similarly, pleasant attendance of events like concerts due to the development of a temporary sense of sharing among attendees leads them to return frequently to similar events more than the content of the happening itself (Jahn et al., 2018). Since being present at an event is considered to be a liminal experience as it is a short-lived break from consolidated routines and social order, it is quite notable that reiterated liminality is connected to the formation of a communitas in this case. Reliance and enjoyment of spontaneous and egalitarian ties lay the foundations for undertaking transitions again over time. Liminality can then be interpreted as a 'routine liminality' that tends to be recursive, without implying modification of state or role. As Wilhoit (2017, p. 266) argued concerning commuting as a repeated liminal experience, the concept of routine liminality refers to 'situations in which liminality happens with regularity, yet maintains the ambiguity and transitional elements of liminality.'

The observation and related conceptualization of the reiteration of liminal experiences has raised the issue of the 'liminality muscle' or 'liminality competence.' Facing transitions becomes a competence that individuals develop and that helps them cope with passages with increasing ease (Borg and Söderlund, 2015; Ibarra and Obodaru, 2016; Wilhoit, 2017; Söderlund and Borg, 2018). The idea that the ability to cope with liminality might reinforce its potential benefits and reduce its drawbacks is a relevant contribution offered by recent reflection on liminality in organizational contexts. One can learn to handle liminal experiences as well as technical skills. Growing a liminal competence or muscle is an outcome of liminality that ensues from repetitiveness of transitions and in turn informs further our understanding of the learning processes related to these experiences. As Ibarra and Obodaru (2016, p. 60) stated, 'people can develop a "liminality muscle," such that the more they are exposed to liminality, the better equipped they are to deal with and make the most of it.' This learning effect, which differs from the traditional learning of work-oriented competencies, raises a question that will be addressed in Chapter 4: if liminality becomes familiar as it consists of a series of subsequent episodes, do individuals still feel to be 'betwixt and between' when they experience another passage? Do they still face a disruption of established social order and engage in identity work to make sense of who they are and who they might become? To sum up, is repeated liminality—but the same doubt applies to permanent liminality—still liminality?

Liminality as a Dynamic Experience

The temporal aspect of liminality that is under scrutiny brings to the fore the dynamic nature of liminality. Transitions can in fact begin in a recognizable way (i.e., a temporary work assignment or the diagnosis of a physical disease) and gradually evolve into new forms according to often unpredictable trajectories. The initial situation is modified and the experience of liminality wanders off the point, marking a distance from any expectations.

The inner dynamism undergirding liminality is only partially caught by the reference to its processual nature made by Söderlund and Borg (2018). Liminality as a process in fact has been related to temporal liminality, i.e., with a phenomenon that is due to finish: 'liminality is associated with a passing, transitional and temporary condition' (Söderlund and Borg, 2018, p. 894). By stressing the dynamism of liminality, the possibility for a given liminal experience to turn into a different type of experience is instead taken into account.

Evolutionary patterns of liminality can be aptly grasped in some studies in the health field. Meaningful evidence is yielded by research on cancer patients (Little et al., 1998; Adorno, 2015). Individuals are first ushered through the threshold between well-being and sickness by a cancer diagnosis: this gives rise to an acute liminal stage, in which treatments entail a perception of suspension filled with hope between the former normal life as a healthy person and a yet uncertain future. An intense identity work takes place at this point in which bonds with other people facing a similar adversity play a relevant role in carving out a possible 'new self' (Adorno, 2015). While ties with fellow patients give rise to a communitas, a widening gap can come into being with former relationships that turn out to be unable to provide empathy and support throughout the healing process. This liminal experience is likely to lead to further liminality, whatever its endpoint might be. If there is a recovery and patients enter remission, they may feel to remain in a situation of uncertainty about future health that is heightened whenever routine examinations and medical checkups take place (Del Vecchio-Good, Good, Schaffer, and Lind, 1990; Charmaz and Belgrave, 2013). In the worst scenario of becoming terminally ill, individuals and their families are called to face still another type of liminality: 'patients' self-narratives disaggregate within this space, as the cancer patient learns to *unbecome* as a cancer patient to a yet unknown self-narrative' (Adorno, 2015, p. 105, italics in the original). In this unfortunate evolution, individuals cope with the difficulty to be 'ill (i.e. no longer well), not expected to recover, but not yet deceased' (McClement and Woodgate, 1997, p. 301).

Liminality can therefore be multifaceted and change its nature as the transition unfolds. With regard to the original elaboration of liminality offered by Victor Turner, the compelling evidence on transitions in the health field shows that their endpoint can be neither a different state or position nor the reincorporation in the previous order, but a nuanced, yet different, type of passage. The different experiences portrayed in the studies on cancer-stricken patients share a kernel of liminality: people are fraught with anxiety and uncertainty, but can also feel a sense of growth and transcendence.

In a related vein, the research carried out by Brown et al. (2017) on individuals suffering from chronic diseases expanded on the possible transformation of liminality. Patients of long-term illnesses, which are often of a psychological nature and hard to be accurately diagnosed by physicians and accepted by relatives, friends, and colleagues, encounter a first liminal experience due to not being healthy anymore, but not overtly and officially sick yet. Once that a correct diagnosis is finally achieved, liminality takes on a new shape: individuals perceive, and are perceived, to be ill, torn between the awareness of 'who they used to be, but no longer are' and the uncertainty about 'who they will become.' If health conditions improve, liminality varies again: people in recovery are often denied acknowledgment, especially by others with whom they have built a communitas based on a common journey and fate (Grue, 2014). At this point, as the authors unraveled, a sense of suspension stems from the realization that individuals are not sick anymore, but not even fully healthy again. It is notable that three nuanced liminal experiences then surface from the stories told by Brown and coauthors (2017) about people fighting against chronic diseases: first, liminality as being neither healthy nor sick, followed by liminality as being sick, i.e., no longer healthy and not recovered yet, and finally liminality as not being sick anymore, but not healthy yet.

Changing the nature of the transition within the same journey brings a still different view on liminality compared not only to its initial theorization, but also to the duration of liminality discussed above: liminality can be a series of subsequent, interrelated indeterminateness whose only the starting point is known—being initially well, in this case. This emergent perspective on liminality as a chain of interwoven experiences reminds us of the metaphor used by Douglas (1966) to describe dangerous creatures crossing the threshold between purity and danger, between ethical behaviors and the pursuit of opportunistic interests: individuals who become 'liminal in a new sense' (Brown et al., 2017, p. 706) remain in a situation of suspension in the long run, but the shape and unfolding of suspension is subject to continuous transformation, passing through various physical and metaphorical borders. Liminality can in the end be seen as permanent, but with different meanings, attitudes, and outcomes over time.

Liminality as Additive Experiences

The revision of the core features of liminality—the time aspect above all—offered by research in heterogenous fields has raised another relevant point, i.e., the possibility to be simultaneously engaged in more liminal experiences within a single or in different domains. We might call this 'multiple or additive liminality,' as it engenders the feeling of being in transition in more spheres simultaneously. Individuals can be temporary workers, while going through a divorce, or being sick and a consultant at the same time. Various forms of liminality are likely to pile up, making the interpretation of passages multifaceted and complex.

The reflection by Szakolczai (2009) brings to the foreground multiple liminality embodied in history ensuing from concurrent social and individual transitions. The situation of the youngest generations of soldiers during the First and Second World Wars has been interpreted through the lens of additive liminality, as Pritchard and Morgan (2006) also claimed. Those born between 1895 and 1900 and between 1920 and 1927 found themselves struggling with a double transition: that corresponding to their quitting civil life, made of affective ties, studies, and occupations, and that corresponding to the societal change from peace and order to war and precariousness. A significant individual disruption matches in this case major societal turmoil or 'social drama.' The anxiety and uncertainty related to the personal condition are amplified by the fears and stress stemming from macro-level upheaval.

Multiple liminal experiences can be lived across professional and personal spheres as well. Kirk, Bal, and Janssen (2017) recounted the complex trajectories of Indian highly skilled male professionals in the fields of engineering, IT, consultancy, and management who moved to the Netherlands to work for international companies. In leaving their country to settle down in a foreign country, the migrants under study were exposed to plural liminal experiences at the same time. They lived far from home in an unfamiliar space that was perceived as both fascinating and threatening, unaware whether and how they would be incorporated into the local community. They were attracted by the freedom from social constraints that they enjoyed and the curiosity for alternative ways of living that stood in marked contrast with the habits they were used to back at home. As Kirk and coauthors (2017, p. 2777) reported, their informants acknowledge 'both a sense of distance and not-belonging, and of adventure and new experiences' when reasoning about their condition as expats.

The feeling of being in transition due to the physical distance from a familiar culture (in spite of remaining in constant touch with family and friends in India) and the exposure to a new one is made more acute by the intention to relocate sometime soon to places that offer better job opportunities like the United States or United Kingdom. An additional form of liminality overlapping with the sensation of being 'betwixt and between' the Eastern and Western worlds can be traced back to professionals' personal state as bachelors subjected to strong expectations to get married: their single—sometimes lonely, often exciting—life in Amsterdam is seen as a temporary transition between the family life conducted in India with parents and siblings and the impending family life as married men that has been in many cases already planned for them. The stories recounted by these authors cast light on the twofold liminality simultaneously experimented by Indian knowledge workers living abroad: the former is multifaceted and refers to life between home and host country, upon which the perspective of moving again impinges, and the latter regards the lingering between single and married life.

Evidence on double liminality concerning both work and personal sphere is offered also by Winkler and Mahmood (2015). Temporary agency workers are not only oscillating between different assignments, client companies, and workplaces, but they often feel 'put on hold' even in their private lives. Spending long periods away from partners and children, in distant cities, going through a great deal of lonely time, especially in the evening, drives people to be puzzled, feeling in between family and solo life, 'neither here nor there.' Regarding the dual liminality perceived by the professionals that they studied, Winkler and Mahmood (2015, p. 63) claimed that 'the work life sheds into the private life, making the private life-zone one where the temporary agency workers experience their liminal situation as well.' It is worth underlining that a clear causal relationship is reported in this case of temporary work: liminality in the work domain prompts additional liminality in the private domain. It is plausible, however, that multiple liminality might be the outcome of quasi-independent situations or events, such as facing an affective loss while undergoing the merger of the employing company with another one.

Additive liminality can unfold within a same domain, too. The dual liminality that is ascribed to the project managers investigated by Hodgson and Paton (2016) described in Chapter 2 testifies to this occurrence. Professionals are argued to be in the middle of various logics that can turn out to be contradictory, entailing a sense of bafflement and ambiguity. Project managers feel to be affiliated with both the company they work for and the international professional community of project managers. At the same time, they are ambivalent about the technical and the managerial bulk of their job. Consequently, they are '"twice-liminal"; first, caught in the space between identification as a cosmopolitan and as a locally oriented professional; and second, caught in the transition between technical professional and managerial professional' (Hodgson and Paton, 2016, p. 30).

Recognizing multiple or additive liminality as developing in a single domain or in more domains can problematize Ibarra and Obodaru's (2016, p. 59) assumption that 'liminality refers to suspension between identities occupying the same identity space (e.g., two work identities, two gender identities, two cultural identities).' If this interpretation holds true and is clarifying when a single form of liminality is at play, it weakens when an individual is involved in two or more forms of liminality. This avenue cries out for more research, however. Multiple liminality is in fact as reasonable and appealing as a still overlooked perspective in organizational reflection. In spite of the surprising paucity of studies addressing plural liminal experiences lived by an individual, Szakolczai's (2009, p. 159) following assertion that liminality may be cumulative and additive and, as such, likely more impactful than traditionally conceived of, sounds perfectly convincing:

> Liminality, however, is not only cumulative over time (meaning that the effects of several liminal situations reinforce each other), but also additive at the point of emergence (meaning that a combination of liminal aspects produces a particularly strong impact). Situations that are liminal in more ways than one might produce particularly strong effects.

Liminality as Degree of Intensity of Experience

An interesting and quite plausible view on liminality that has been raised, but treated only theoretically thus far, regards the possibility of nuances or degrees of this experience. The undergirding idea is that a liminal experience may be a matter of degrees of feeling to be in a 'gray area' rather than a dichotomy between being or not in such a situation. In other words, transitions cannot be reduced to 'being or not being liminal' at a given point, but to how much in suspension individuals perceive to be. This reflection paves the way for a subtler interpretation of the concept of liminality, such that being a consultant, a migrant, or a person undergoing treatments to recover from a disease does not necessarily imply equivalent feelings of being 'betwixt and between.'

The call for a more refined elaboration of liminality has been variously expressed in different spheres. In delving into liminality, Thomassen (2015) proposed that liminality be distinguished according to different dimensions. The temporal dimension refers to specific moments (e.g., expected or unexpected events), periods (e.g., weeks or months), or epochs (e.g., generations or decades). The spatial dimension can address specific physical thresholds (e.g., a doorway or the boundaries between sacred and profane places), areas or zones (e.g., airport waiting zones or prisons), or countries and territories (e.g., Palestine or war areas). Liminality can also involve subjects at different levels: individuals, social groups (e.g., adolescents or minorities), or entire populations or societies. In addition to these dimensions, Thomassen (2015, p. 50) introduced a fourth one, i.e., scale or 'the degree to which liminality is experienced—in other words, the intensity of liminal moment or period.' The author explained the intensity of liminality in terms of the convergence of more dimensions of liminality, as is the case when liminality in personal life (e.g., facing a divorce) matches societal changes (e.g., a revolt breaking out) and spaces change (e.g., moving to a temporary location). The scale of liminality has been purposefully described as follows (p. 50, italics in the original):

> Sometimes, however, liminal experiences are intensified as the personal, group, and societal levels converge in liminality, over extended periods of time, or even within several spatial entities. In other words, whereas most experiences of liminality are circumscribed by some kind of *frame*, certain other experiences come closer to "pure liminality", bringing both personal and collective, and spatial and temporal coordinates into play. This neither can nor should be expressed mathematically, but it does seem meaningful to suggest that there exist degrees of liminality.

The need to go beyond a monolithic view on liminality as a property of a given state or role is advanced also by Winkler and Mahmood (2015). They drew from Thomassen's (2009) analysis of liminal dimensions to outline some instances of temporary work. The end of a project may represent a time when the perception of in-betweenness is particularly high for project workers. In a related vein, the realization not to be invited to the client companies' most prominent social events like Christmas parties intensifies temporary workers' feeling to be 'neither here nor there,' but only temporarily affiliated to organizations.

A similar stance was taken by Shortt (2015) and Vesala and Tuomi-vaara (2018) who acknowledged that there can be nuances in liminal experiences. In the case of professionals undertaking a week off from work to spend in an archipelago to elaborate on alternative work practices, individuals' degree of in-betweenness is traced back to two conditions. The former is the novelty that the permanence in a secluded island assumes compared with regular life, while the latter refers to the personal driver for change that leads to embrace or, alternatively, trivialize the ambiguity associated with this experience. Similarly, in recounting hairdressers' usage of liminal spaces in the workplace like stairwells and doorways, Shortt (2015) disclosed how a sense of attachment or stability developed during their regular usage led to 'question if they continue to be either "liminal" or just "spaces" at all' (p. 639). In other words, the degree of liminality decreases as the meaning of spaces evolves through their recurrent use.

Degree or intensity of liminality can be linked to the liminality 'muscle' or competence described above (Ibarra and Obodaru, 2016; Söderlund and Borg, 2018). Reiterating liminal experiences allows to nurture individual skills to cope with liminality that can gradually lessen the degree of feeling to be 'neither here nor there.' As experiences of liminality pile up over time, within a single domain or across domains, being in transition may become a regular pattern of being, and its intensity likely wane.

Liminality as Creation of Practices

Contributions from various domains point to liminal experiences as the opportunity to fill the void generated by the fading of established social order with new practices at an individual, group, and organizational level. In Chapter 3, individual agency has been dealt with as a relevant feature of liminality in organizational contexts. There are burgeoning evidence and speculation in yet other fields that individuals make sense of and shape their transitions through the enactment of behaviors that tend to be recursive across liminal experiences. Once again, liminality in contemporary society points to the centrality of individuals over the collective (Söderlund and Borg, 2018). Individual practices serve the primary function to reduce ambiguity and to draw liminars nearer to the normal life conducted by those who are not undergoing any passages.

Often practices take on the sacred nature of rituals that are repeated regularly, even daily or more times a day, to gain control over life when uncertainty is high, as Hoel Felde (2011, p. 606) affirmed: 'The ritualized strategies provide a sense of control over the uncertain existence in the fluid, ambiguous and dangerous, socially abnormal liminal space of living.' Instances from heterogeneous domains testify to the resort to individual rituals to find relief and diminish anxiety related to transitions and that this tendency is reinforced when liminality is protracted over time. Significant hints for a greater comprehension of individual agency are offered by studies in the health sphere. Individuals with high cholesterol are medically sick, but apparently in good shape, which poses them in an intermediate 'gray zone' between illness and well-being (Hoel Felde, 2011). They set up repeated practices or rituals to continuously navigate the passages from medical treatments to ordinary life, such as 'cheating on the diet' but claiming to 'do everything in moderation.' Their narratives show how they alternate healthy and proper food with more enjoyable and tastier food, provided that they eat less of the latter than of the former, within the same day, how they cook normal and low-fat versions of the same food to accommodate dietary restrictions with family obligations when preparing home meals, or how they draw boundaries between compliance with medical requirements at home and reasonable indulgence when going out with friends. Recursive patterns of action and usage of spaces and artifacts, such as home kitchens, restaurants, ingredients, and cooking tools, become routines that help individuals affected by chronic illness 'produce and reproduce shared worlds of meaning from ambiguous situations; rituals create social bonds, reincorporating the cholesterol subject in the social world' (Hoel Felde, 2011, p. 606).

Individual tactics for self-recovery in the wake of chronic disease are reported by Brown et al. (2017), too. Self-help and self-informing initiatives targeting beneficial diets and drugs, as well as daily gauging the percentage of recovery perceived or physical activity undertaken and doing meditation, match a sensemaking rhetoric based on statements like 'People have to find their own way' and 'It may not work for everybody' (p. 703).

In another health-related context, that of cancer survivorship, the biographical work in which individuals are engaged tells about the sensation to be suspended between who they used to be before falling sick and who they will become after cancer is behind them (Blows et al., 2012). Rituals that patients in remission adopt are aimed at signaling healing from acute sickness and ongoing transformation into a recovered person, and rely on meaningful symbols, such as writing notes on the journey accomplished and burning them out, or sowing seed of plants and cater to their growth (Sleight, 2016). These rituals differ from those related to re-covery pathways described by Hoel Felde (2011) in that, although they remain strictly personal, they are deployed during psycho-logical therapies aimed at helping people overcome their traumas. Consequently, they are shared with therapists and not applied out of purely individual design and intention. Put differently, there is a social endeavor matching individual practices.

Interestingly, rituals meant to mark the relinquishing of a pre-vious identity and the embracing of a new one tend to follow the process that accompanies any psychologically safe transitions: first, a 'letting-go' phase in which old identities are dropped has to be gone through. Subsequently, opposite emotions and impulses are felt (wandering), which give way to the elaboration of a new vision of self in the future (new beginning). Eventually, the prospective vision is integrated into real life, thus engendering a change in the self-concept (Sleight, 2016).

Evidence of practices created by individuals extends beyond the health domain, however. Commuters and travelers testify to the ability, and the necessity as well, to navigate a liminal situation through the construction and the use of personal routines. Com-muters are shown to carve out their own practices to manage a re-current liminality that consists in their regular trips back and forth from home to the workplace and fit them into the rest of their work and personal life (Nippert-Eng, 2008; Wilhoit, 2017). Commuting is shaped as alone time, and a break from the social norms individ-uals must comply with in the spaces they inhabit. The suspension that driving a car or riding a train engenders becomes an opportu-nity to mentally relax and take a distance from daily obligations, catch up with unfinished work, or nourish passions like reading books, listening to music, or knitting. The variety of activities that commuting workers commit to when they are neither at work nor at home turn timelessness into valued, productive time conveying meaning to both realms, while normalizing repeated transitions.

In a similar vein, while waiting to board planes, travelers play out shopping 'rituals,' like buying unusual drinks, snacks, or gifts, or patterns of actions that are associated with this experience, such as watching people and exercising imagination to guess their stories, daydreaming, or initiating conversations with strangers (Kociat-kiewicz and Kostera, 2011; Huang et al., 2018). Repeating liminality routines when traveling helps individuals handle the anxiety and fear ensuing from the loss of previous habits, spaces, and social in-teractions, and the uncertainty about what may loom over their trip.

Different individual practices are enacted by Indian professionals living abroad who, as previously seen, are deemed to be twice-liminal, since they have left their country behind without reaching the final destination and are also positioned between their former family ties and an impending life as married persons (Kirk et al. 2017). Food-related routines act as a means to manage the twofold transition that they live: some of them prefer cooking Indian dishes to feel closer to their home country, whereas others conversely stress how they like tasting alternative cuisines to take a distance from their roots and embrace the new perspectives that their temporary location offers.

At a team level, the creation of practices has been underlined, once again in the health domain, by the new routines that a hospital staff can introduce to tackle an unforeseen event. In their analysis of the reaction against the spread of an epidemy that represented a major disruption in extant operations and opened up a transition towards an uncertain scenario, Teo, Lee, and Lim (2017) unraveled the practices that emergency team members jointly construed to speed up diagnosis and reduce likelihood of infection, such as simplifying hierarchical reports and decoupling task assignments from seniority. Similarly, instances of teams' generation of practices were conveyed for boards of directors (Concannon and Nordberg, 2018). Boardrooms are considered as liminal spaces since they are only temporarily occupied, are located neither internally nor externally to the company, are detached from the regular workplaces inhabited by organizational members, and rule out hierarchy among team members in favor of an egalitarian stance. Faced with increasing pressure towards institutionalization through compliance with regulation and law that might penalize service to the company, directors instead communicated the preference that they accorded to service through shared informal practices. Examples of these practices are the organization sof 'strategy away days' to reflect on strategic issues without distractions, social events like lunches or dinners that entail further conversations in the boardroom, or meetings with stakeholders. In line with the creative outcomes ensuing from liminality, boardrooms become liminal spaces in which directors can sharpen their wits sustaining their strategizing beyond formal expectations and legal requirements and fitting team orientation and interests.

Finally, liminality is argued to generate practices also at an organizational level. Particularly meaningful evidence is yielded by the study on migrants carried out by Richter (2016). Confined in camps, suspended between the home that they have quit and the destination that they are unable to reach, migrants recreate a social structure that, by means of the emergent roles and routines, provides them with some stability and guidance. The establishment of a 'ghetto system,' with its 'law of the ghetto' and 'ghetto tax' prescribing appropriate behaviors to follow, is a proxy for political government in the 'gray area' in which migrants dwell. Not only must codified practices be complied with by members of the ghetto, but sometimes grotesque symbolism and rituals mark allegiance to the system, such as government meetings regularly taking place in the ironically dubbed 'White House,' which is just a larger tent in an alien and aloof environment (Table 3.1).

Table 3.1 Emergent perspectives on liminality

Emergent feature	Main characteristics	Main references
Liminality as protracted experience	Liminality may become permanent or even a limbo	Ibarra and Obodaru (2016); Bamber et al. (2017); Söderlund and Borg (2018)
Liminality as repeated experience	Liminality as a series of experiences unfolding over time Temporary incorporation Enactment of a routine liminality Development of a liminality 'muscle' or competence	Cohen (2011); Atkinson and Robson (2012); Bui et al. (2014); Ibarra and Obodaru (2016); Jahn et al. (2018); Ryan (2019)
Liminality as dynamic experience	Liminality as continuously and unforeseeably evolving	Little et al. (1998); Adorno (2015); Brown et al. (2017)
Liminality as additive or multiple experiences	Plural simultaneous liminal experiences lived at both the individual and social levels, in both the work and private life spheres, or within a single sphere	Pritchard and Morgan (2006); Szakolczai (2009); Winkler and Mahmood (2015); Kirk et al. (2017)
Liminality as degree of intensity of experience	Intensity of liminal experiences influenced by their occurrence across different dimensions (subject, time, and space)	Thomassen (2009, 2015); Shortt (2015); Winkler and Mahmood (2015); Vesala and Tuomivaara (2018)
Liminality as creation of practices	Individual, group, and organizational practices to cope with liminality	Hoedl Felde (2011); Sleight (2016); Brown et al. (2017); Richter (2016); Wilhoit (2017)

Conclusion

The growing interest that liminality has been endlessly encountering in heterogeneous fields has prompted a revision of some of its core features, while proposing additional views, as is shown in *Table 3.1*. As a consequence, the perspective on liminality becomes richer, but at the same time, its original, powerful message is somewhat diluted by subsequent integrations. A major assumption that has been questioned regards the temporal dimension of liminal experiences in contemporary society. Liminality being a transition due to have a limited duration and to finish with the acquisition of a new state or role has been probed: experiences of in-betweenness can be prolonged, even bound to last indeterminately, up to the point that they have been likened to a limbo (e.g., Ibarra and Obodaru, 2016; Bamber et al., 2017).

Time is taken into account longitudinally, too: liminal experiences can be repeated over time, thus spurring interesting hints. If liminality can be a series of transitions interrupted by limited returns to normalcy, then incorporation into social order is only short-lived and individuals may develop the capability to handle frequent changes of state or position, called 'liminality muscle' or 'liminality competence' (e.g., Atkinson and Robson, 2012; Ryan, 2019). The growth of a liminality muscle likely lessens the negative effects of feeling 'betwixt and between' and enhances its beneficial contributions. Reducing emphasis on liminality as a process unfolding in a given time lapse brings in unprecedented dynamism: characteristics and meanings of liminality can evolve from an initial onset to a continuous morphing of the experience, without a clear-cut demarcation, as studies in the health domain have disclosed (e.g., Adorno, 2015; Brown, et al., 2017).

More liminal experiences can also be lived in parallel according to an additive pathway that cuts across work and private life or occurs within just one of these spheres (e.g., Thomassen, 2009; Shortt, 2015). Individuals can then feel a sense of suspension both in their personal life choices and in work arrangements, or both in their personal choices and at a higher societal level. As a consequence of the manifold view of liminality that comes up from the previous contributions, the belief that different degrees or nuances of liminality can be acknowledged in an apparently similar situation, such as being in remission after a battle with cancer or a young backpacker traveling abroad for months, is raised.

Finally, going beyond the time issue, a common thread linking the studies examined in this chapter is the relevance assumed by individual, group, or organizational reactions to liminality in less institutionalized contexts like the contemporary society. The construction of practices to cope with the suspension that liminal experiences prompt emerges in different contexts and across heterogeneous fields: the elaboration and enactment of practices that diminish stress and anxiety, often producing even positive effects, can be gleaned at an individual level, such as the routines set up by commuters or travelers during their trips (Wilhoit, 2017; Huang et al., 2018), at a collective level, as is the case with hospital teams handling large-scale emergencies (Teo et al., 2017), and at an organizational level, as happens in migration camps where new roles, rules, and routines are converged upon and become a shared reference for action (Richter, 2016). The construction of practices in the wake of a perception of in-betweenness may account for the creativity expected of liminal experiences, and reinforce the likelihood of liminal experiences to be able to fill the void that they engender. This finding is aligned with, and sheds light on, the assertion that 'While liminality is "unstructure," a lack of fixed points in a given moment, it must at the same time be considered the *origin* of structure' (Thomassen, 2009, p. 23, italics in original).

Honing in on these recent refinements and extensions proposed in various fields, liminality becomes a truly multifaceted construct. While it gains in depth, maybe appealing to a significantly wider audience than the initial anthropological community, it risks, however, losing its essence and blurring the distinction with other constructs, thereby reducing its explanatory power of human behavior, as will be discussed in the next and final chapter.

4   Towards a Model of Liminal Experience

Introduction

The journey along the development of the reflection on liminality in various fields of knowledge is fascinating, albeit puzzling, and calls now for some systematization. Moving away from the original, clear conceptualization offered by Victor Turner, which has been examined in Chapter 1, studies in the organizational domain as well as in other domains have embraced with growing enthusiasm the liminal lens to investigate a wide range of phenomena. After decades of burgeoning attention towards this construct, one is left, however, with as much richness and heterogeneity of perspectives as perplexity about what liminality may *really* be about. Ibarra and Obodaru (2016) cautioned us about the possible alternative constructs that can be mistaken for liminality. According to Ibarra and Obodaru (2016) in fact, in organization research, liminality must be carefully distinguished from other identity-related constructs such as identity conflict and identity ambiguity. Identity conflict can affect two or more identities (e.g., personal and professional identities) that are at odds with each other because their undergirding values and beliefs are inconsistent and convey contrasting references for action, whereas identity ambiguity refers to the labels and the meanings of the values and beliefs of a given identity (e.g., organizational identity) being fuzzy (Corley and Gioia, 2004).

While the exercise of stressing differences from other concepts reinforces the construct under consideration, some drifts lately addressed in research on liminality may undermine the benefits of this exercise, turning virtually every social phenomenon into a possible liminal experience. Some contributions that have been analyzed in the preceding chapter as a matter of fact lessen the clarity of this construct. Especially calling into question the temporal dimension may end up weakening our understanding of liminality. If it is plausible that transitions become longer, with separation and incorporation being more nuanced in a scarcely institutionalized society, the permanence attributed to some transitions may be not only an oxymoron, but even potentially misleading. However long transitions might be, the essence of liminality is that of being a stage of *suspension* between a 'before' and an 'after,' or in-betweenness. This interpretation is shared by the most robust studies on this topic. Turner (1967, pp. 96–97) summed up the gist of liminality stating that it is about being 'neither one thing nor another, or maybe both.' Along a similar line of reasoning, Bamber, Allen-Collinson, and McCormack (2017) synthesized liminality as a limbo that ties individuals to an undesired situation: they feel to be always here (unpleasant position) and never there (wished-for position).

When talking about liminality, it is necessary that there are a 'here' and a 'there,' a 'this' and a 'that,' and a 'before' and an 'after,' which can be more or less clear, more or less enticing, and more or less close in time, but nevertheless demark a suspension perceived by individuals between a former state or role and a later one. This tenet of liminality has to be kept in mind to properly employ the concept to comprehend human behaviors, feelings, and thoughts. It is not sufficient to be aware to have left something behind and entered a 'gray zone' to frame an experience within the liminal discourse: some state or role must lie ahead towards which to tender, no matter whether and when they will be attained or how obscure they might seem if thought about while living the transition. Otherwise, any uncertainty and ambiguity that can be felt in human life *become* liminality. This risk calls for the necessity to retrieve Turner's original, meaningful theorization. In order for an experience to resonate for liminality, it has to be perceived as a transition *and* it has to comprise some or all of the founding elements of liminality, namely spacelessness, timelessness, rituals, anti-structure, communitas, and identity work. In revamping the vision of liminality advanced by anthropology, hints ensuing from its observation in contemporary contexts will be integrated and discussed in the following sections.

Perception of Liminal Experience

The latest contributions to liminality have highlighted how liminal experiences can accrue over time, prompting the development of a 'liminality muscle' or 'liminal competence' (Ibarra and Obodaru, 2016; Wilhoit, 2017; Söderlund and Borg, 2018). The capability to face new forms of liminality in contemporary life implies that the impact of subsequent exposure likely be modified and that transitioning be assimilated to an ordinary way of living. Liminal experiences are also dynamic throughout their development, and can unfold simultaneously in the work and personal life domains, or just in one of them (Szakolczai, 2009; Brown, Huszar, and Chapman, 2017; Kirk, Bal, and Janssen, 2017). The degree of intensity of liminal experiences and their characteristics (spacelessness, timelessness, rituals, anti-structure, communitas, identity work) are expected to change as the competence to deal with transitions grows, in the different moments of the transition, and according to the multiplicity of transitions simultaneously gone through (Sturdy, Schwarz, and Spicer, 2006; Vesala and Tuomivaara, 2018).

In light of this reasonable expectation, liminality as a static attribute of a given state or role—being a consultant, a cancer-stricken patient in remission, or a frequent traveler—has to be revised. For instance, if professionals choose to remain consultants long, they can gradually see their work at the boundaries between the consulting company and the client company as an ordinary positioning or their *raison d'etre* at work. Although rituals and symbols marking the different phases may be repeated whenever a new project is carried out (Czarniawska and Mazza, 2003), their incremental effect is probably attenuated and working at the edge is no longer lived as a disruptive suspension, but a familiar way of being and acting, so much so that identity work becomes a marginal engagement. Relatedly, even within a single consulting company, it is realistic that members do not have the same experience of transitioning, which is likely differently articulated in terms of liminal elements for junior consultants and for their senior colleagues accustomed to start, perform, complete, and restart projects. The influence of rites, the sensation of inhabiting unusual spaces, while being governed by unusual rhythms, and the revision of the sense of self are expected to be stronger for the former than for the latter. Even though they are all consultants, their liminal experiences can be quite heterogeneous, even variable from time to time. For the same individual in fact, e.g., a seasoned consultant, liminal experiences can be differently shaped throughout the transition: placelessness can be higher at the beginning of a project to be then lessened, and anti-structure can be gradually shared with members of the client company.

Time is ripe then for comprehending individuals' *perception of liminal experience*, instead of acknowledging the association between a certain role (e.g., an interorganizational network manager or a consultant) or state (e.g., a chronically ill patient or a migrant in a detention camp), and liminality. It is individuals that are in transition who have to recognize and voice the characteristics of their in-betweenness, and not the researchers who are interested in studying liminality. A dichotomic view of liminality—liminar and non-liminar—embraces a surprisingly simplified view of liminality as a property that is held (or not held) according to the researcher. Conversely, Turner's theorization of liminality deeply elaborated on how liminality is perceived and enacted through space, time, rituals, anti-structure, communitas, and identity work. While liminality can undoubtedly benefit from the perspectives reported in Chapters 2 and 3, it still mostly points instead to a static interpretation as a property of a state or role. This is likely due to the fact that empirical studies on liminality are mostly qualitative (e.g., Kornberger, Justesen, and Mouritsen, 2011; Shortt, 2015; Vesala and Tuomivaara, 2018; Ryan, 2019) and are based upon a common premise: analyzing specific aspects of liminality (e.g., individual practices, learning, or stress and fears) in a setting that is *a priori* considered to be homogeneously liminal, such as an Information System design project, a workshop in a secluded island, or the position of manager in an accounting firm. Grasping liminal experiences requires a different approach to liminality: it has not to be taken for granted, but investigated through interviews or through an appropriate scale, whose necessity has been already evoked (Ibarra and Obodaru, 2016), to realize whether individuals do feel in transition and what features their liminal experiences take on.

The perception of liminal experiences, which can then differ for individuals in one and the same state or role and throughout the process, can be comprehended through the very core features theorized by Victor Turner, which are revised below in light of the subsequent integrations suggested by the studies that have been examined in the Chapters 2 and 3, highlighting the dimensions of each of them. Unlike Turner's account, we now know that not all of them must be present in a liminal experience nor are they always the same along the way.

The Dimensions of Timeliness and Spacelessness

Based on the belief that liminality is a suspension between a 'before' and an 'after' and between a 'here' and a 'there,' timelessness and spacelessness as core elements of this experience can be elaborated further thanks to the contributions that have been delved into in the preceding chapters.

Timelessness can be refined according to the following three dimensions:

Change of time flow: Entering the 'gray zone' calls for modifying work and life rhythms (Vesala and Tuomivaara, 2018). Time does not flow as it used to nor as it still does for those who are not facing a liminal experience: the perception of daily activities' time span changes significantly and the comparison with previous familiar ways to spend time is constantly in liminars' mind (Hoel Felde, 2011; Brown et al., 2017). The altered pace of time pertained to original studies on liminality: in his various writings, Turner (e.g., 1967, 1969) underlined how life abides by different temporal rules when undergoing transitions from those applying to individuals in ordinary situations.

Blurred temporal boundaries: The distinction between activities tend to fade away in liminal experiences. Individual and collective activities, but also different work tasks, and even work and leisure activities are intermingled, and individuals find it hard to tell the beginning, the duration, and the end of the activities they are engaged in (Vesala and Tuomivaara, 2018; Ryan, 2019). As Vesala and Tuomivaara (2018) stressed, losing temporal constraints can allow liminars to gain freedom, embrace new perspectives, and be more creative.

Transition length: Speculation on liminality has been increasingly proposing longer liminal experiences, which have even been posited to become permanent (Ibarra and Obodaru, 2016; Bamber et al., 2017). The perception of being in between a 'before' and an 'after' can last significantly longer than for the transitions investigated by Turner. The stretching of the temporal boundaries of transitions needs to be included in the timelessness dimension, although permanence in a state or role might, as argued above, no longer be a liminal experience if there is no tension perceived towards an 'after,' however distant and confused it may be.

Concerning spacelessness, three dimensions have emerged thus far in the literature that are commented below.

Change of space: Liminal experiences are accompanied and underscored by a change of the spaces usually inhabited. The loss of familiar locations pertains to the transitions of migrants leaving their country with the goal of building a new life abroad, parents supporting children with special needs throughout rehabilitation programs, teams trying to reach the Himalaya summit, or professionals adhering to creative workshops in remote islands (e.g., Cohn, 2001; Tempest, Starkey, and Ennew, 2007; Richter, 2016; Vesala and Tuomivaara, 2018). Liminality is therefore associated with dwelling in the new physical environments where suspension is felt.

Space ambiguity: The new spaces that liminality opens up to are often hard to decipher and to appropriate. Unlike liminal experiences in the anthropological realm, which are associated with specific places through the celebration of rituals, in many recent instances, liminars juggle their activities in different locations, oscillating between more and less familiar settings. People facing acute or chronic diseases combine attendance of usual locations, such as home and offices, with peculiar tangible or virtual ones, such as hospitals, online communities, or meeting rooms where self-help groups gather (e.g., Grue, 2014; Brown et al., 2017). Similarly, commuters or frequent travelers are used to spending time in only apparently foreign places like airports and trains (Wilhoit, 2017; Huang, Xiao, and Wang, 2018). Through repeated occupation, these settings can cease being psychologically destabilizing or troublesome to become instead a source of ease and inspiration. Even though initially unfamiliar spaces can be interpreted differently over time, a sense of space ambiguity remains which can be expressed as a difficulty to realize where to really belong to or as the sensation to belong to many places and to none in particular.

Separateness: Liminal experiences prompt a distance taken from the spaces in which people who are not facing a transition continue with their established way of living. Sick people find themselves mostly interacting with, and surrounded by, other individuals who are also unwell and by medical staff in recovery-dedicated places (e.g., Brown et al., 2017). In a related vein, survivors of a tragic shooting in a school stuck to each other and carved out 'safe' spaces in which to gather, reason together, and try to overcome what they had lived through the enactment of new routines (Powley, 2009). Additionally, unemployed as well as nascent entrepreneurs developed their business ideas in locations that were alternative to ordinary workplaces (Daniel and Ellis-Chadwick, 2016; Daskalaki and Simosi, 2018). Liminality therefore entails individuals' detachment from familiar spaces to occupy, and sometimes even build and shape, unconventional spaces in which transitions unfold.

The Dimensions of Anti-structure

Liminal experiences are characterized by the breakage of consolidated order with its hierarchy, status recognition, and sets of rules (e.g., Turner, 1974a; Atkinson and Robson, 2012; Hodgson and Paton, 2016). This core feature of liminality can be further distinguished in divergence from extant structures and emergence of a new structure.

Divergence from extant structures: Coping with liminality is intertwined with the erasure or fading of established roles, rules, and procedures that can also turn into an animated contrast (Turner, 1969; Szakolczai, 2009; Pina e Cunha, Guimarães-Costa, Rego, and Clegg, 2010). When inhabiting the 'gray area' or 'twilight zone' to which liminality has been likened, individuals are no longer exposed to the guidance—and to the constraints—that regular structures provide (Reid-Cunningham, 2009; Kornberger et al., 2011). The weakening or complete vanishing of former points of reference, which has been argued by Turner, has been corroborated by research in various fields. Hybrid entrepreneurs who resort to self-storage facilities to develop their business idea, unemployed people who search for alternative jobs, sometimes even founding new ventures, or professionals taking a week-long retreat to elaborate on alternative work processes detach themselves from familiar, albeit somewhat suffocating, patterns of action and interaction (Daniel and Ellis-Chadwick, 2016; Garcia-Lorenzo, Donnelly, Sell-Trujillo, and Imas, 2018; Vesala and Tuomivaara, 2018).

Emergence of a new structure: The fading of consolidated order can make room for the emergence of a new order regulating the liminal experience. Liminality, as already stressed, replaces established structure with alternative points of references: the void is filled with rules, norms, and routines that do not apply to individuals who have not embarked upon a similar pathway (Thomassen, 2009; Kornberger et al., 2011). As recalled earlier, liminality can be the end and, at the same time, the origin of order and structure (Thomassen, 2009; Turner, 1969, 1974a). A new set of rules and positions are created to manage liminal situations: in immigration camps, a hierarchical system endowed with its own symbols is put into place and represents a guidepost for migrants waiting for a final destination (Klein and Williams, 2012; Richter, 2016). Likewise, individuals coping with cancer treatments or long-term diseases submit to new regimes with their own rules and roles to cater to which, while differing from those that healthy people comply with, nonetheless, offer a framework for navigating the transition (Little, Jordens, Paul, Montgomery, and Philipson, 1998; Sleight, 2016; Brown et al., 2017). As Daniel and Ellis-Chadwick (2016) claimed, there can be notable structure and method in liminality.

The Dimensions of Communitas

A distinctive element of liminal experiences that marks the difference between the construct under study and other constructs is the communitas, i.e., the strong, spontaneous ties that link liminars to each other and that often contribute to widen the gap from those who are not handling a transition. Research on liminality has unraveled various dimensions of communitas, namely detachment from previous relationships, egalitarian stance, and distance from non-liminars.

Detachment from previous relationships: When embracing a liminal experience, individuals enter a new realm in which there is little room or comfort with former relationships. From the anthropological origins on, instances of liminality have disclosed the mismatch between liminars and many social connections previously cherished. This may happen out of necessity, as is the case with migrants moving far away from home who are forced to reduce the intensity of contacts with friends and relatives (e.g., Boland, 2013; Richter, 2016), or as a choice, as happens when liminars intend to sideline, at least temporarily, familiar ties to experiment with new patterns of interaction, e.g., when traveling, attending college, or during adolescence (Cody and Lawlor, 2011; Bui, Wilkins, and Lee, 2014; Karioris, 2016).

Egalitarian stance: The deletion of taken-for-granted status and hierarchical positions characterizes liminal experiences, in which a sense of kinship and closeness rather prevail (Murphy, 1987; Atkinson and Robson, 2012). New personal and intimate bonds can be set, nourished, and valued among travelers sharing the same short-term accommodation to which traditional power relations do not apply (Pritchard and Morgan, 2006), as well as among survivors of tragic events who resort to each other to find some relief regardless of their social status or hierarchical position (Powley, 2009). Traditional power maps are ruled out in favor of an emergent comradeship also among unemployed who coalesce to search a way out of their difficult situation or project members affiliated with different organizational units and external consultants during an IS project (Wagner, Newell, and Kay, 2012; Daskalaki and Simosi, 2018).

Distance from non-liminars: Building strong ties with fellows sharing a similar pathway can prompt a gradual sense of separation from those who remain in a well-known situation. Undergoing the change that liminality stirs in fact not only draws individuals who deal with the same sense of suspension closer to each other, but at the same time widens the perception of the difference from people who are unfamiliar with the experience currently lived. The increasing cognitive and behavioral breach that opens between liminars and non-liminars emerges in a particularly compelling way when facing a disease, a disability, or the permanence in an immigration camp or in a detention facility (Murphy, Scheer, Murphy, and Mack, 1988; Murphy, 1995; Moran, 2013; Richter, 2016). The world of 'others' becomes a foreign world, even though it was the realm inhabited for a long time: the alternative spaces, time pace, rules, norms, procedures, and questioning about the self that transitional experiences embody lead liminars to feel separate from those who continue with their habitual lives—as a healthy person, a free person, or regular employee—and to 'close ranks' with individuals who have undertaken a common trajectory and likely share a similar fate, too.

The articulation of the dimensions of a communitas that research on liminality in heterogeneous fields—with the notable exception of most organizational studies—has unraveled significantly enriches one of the prominent and distinctive features of this construct.

The Dimensions of Identity Work

Engagement in identity work to reframe, refine, and embrace a modified self-view represents a core issue in liminality (Caza, Vough, and Puranik, 2018). Reflection on identity work related to liminality has highlighted three different components concerning the process of self-definition: identity loss, identity ambiguity, and identity play.

Identity loss: Undertaking a substantial change requires the letting go of previously held assumptions and beliefs about who one used to be (Conroy and O'Leary-Kelly, 2014). Handling in-betweenness implies in fact the loss of established points of reference, among which a vision of self that was interiorized and likely socially validated, i.e., recognized by knowledgeable others (Swann, Johnson, and Bosson, 2009). A core element of 'being neither one thing nor the other' is in fact that liminars quit the 'one thing' that they would be before embarking on the transition. At that point, individuals, for example, relinquish the healthy person, the family member, or the regular employee that they would be to engage in a passage towards a new state or role (Cohen, 2011; Sleight, 2016; Daskalaki and Simosi, 2018).

Identity ambiguity: Once former identities have lost their significance, individuals are left with a nebulous sense of self. Being 'betwixt and between,' 'neither one thing nor the other,' or maybe both, often entails puzzlement about who one is during the liminal experience: the difficulty to respond to the question 'Who am

I now?' is exacerbated when liminality lasts long or even becomes a limbo whose end is hard to detect (Ibarra and Obodaru, 2016; Bamber et al., 2017).

Identity play: The suspension that is perceived in the sense of self during liminal experiences may be fertile ground for imagining, developing, and testing possible selves to be realized in the future (Ibarra and Petriglieri, 2010; Ibarra and Obodaru, 2016). Quitting long-held identities may represent on one hand a source of destabilization and threat (Petriglieri, 2011), but on the other can free cognitive resources to dedicate to the exploration of self along unusual pathways. This trajectory has been well discerned in individuals who have lost their jobs and, in the wake of the uncertainty that unemployment engenders, start envisaging a future as entrepreneurs that, by availing themselves of the set of relationships that they have built with people in a similar situation, they try to turn into reality (Daskalaki and Simosi, 2018; Garcia-Lorenzo et al., 2018).

Although a strict temporal sequence cannot be identified and an overlap between these three dimensions is likely to occur, identity loss is expected to precede identity ambiguity and identity play, since it denotes the departure from previously held and socially validated identities, followed by puzzlement about the current identity and the beginning of the exploration of possible selves.

The Dimensions of Collective and Individual Practice

Liminality is a suspension between different states or roles that poses cognitive challenges, but is also an opportunity to participate in collective behaviors and to take individual action.

Collective practices: Rites and ceremonies are social practices often associated with liminal experiences. In the original perspective offered by anthropology, starting with the seminal contribution conveyed by Arnold van Gennep (1960), collective moments consisting of formal signs, gestures, accessories, and other visual representations were meant to exhibit the beginning, the unfolding, and the end of transitions. Although rituals have remained mostly confined to the backward of organization studies on this topic, some notable examples have been provided, however. Incorporation and divestiture rites have been reported in projects in various domains, ranging from consultancy to Information Systems and to artistic events organization (Czarniawska and Mazza, 2003; Wagner et al., 2012; Ryan, 2019). More evidence on the convergence among individuals to celebrate transitions is reported in the education field. Graduate and post-graduate programs are conceived of as liminal experiences in which a former, familiar way of living is left behind to prepare for a different, and intentionally better, work future (Wright and Gilmore, 2012; Land, Rattray, and Vivian, 2014; Hawkins and Edwards, 2015). Not only graduation ceremonies, but also orientation weeks, intermediate tests, and final examinations are meant to signal the end of a precedent state and the inception of a new one (Petriglieri and Petriglieri, 2010; Wood, 2012; Karioris, 2016).

Although the de-institutionalization of contemporary societies has lessened the emphasis placed on ceremonies, the formal initiatives that gather liminars at various stages of their transitions remain essential to bring to the fore the social nature of liminality that resides also in the communitas.

Individual practices: Research in other fields than anthropology has pointed to the individual responses and reactions that are enacted to tackle in-betweenness. The emergence of personal ways to deal with liminality is a remarkable contribution conveyed by recent studies on this topic that cuts across various domains, from organization to sociology, and from medicine and health to tourism. Liminars elaborate, play out, negotiate, and refine their own tactics to reduce the stress and anxiety linked to passages, thus enhancing the attainment of benefits from liminality.

Under liminal circumstances, individuals resort to cognitive resources, such as imagining future scenarios for self, fantasizing about others' lives, or revitalizing forgone identities (Wilhoit, 2017; Huang et al., 2018; Ryan, 2019), as well as to enacted behaviors, such as cultivating interests and passions, reconciling different activities, or building a holding environment (Borg and Söderlund, 2015; Swan, Scarbrough, and Ziebro, 2016; Petriglieri, Ashford, and Wrzesniewski, 2019), to make their experience meaningful.

Although collective and individual practices have seldom been coupled in empirical accounts of liminality, the two dimensions are not inconsistent with each other: a liminal experience can comprise shared formal rituals and individual reactivity.

Conclusion

The theorization of liminality originally elaborated by Victor Turner still represents, after many decades, the most solid reference for liminality and the one able to make it a distinctive and fascinating construct among the many proposed in organization studies, such as precariousness, identity ambiguity, and identity conflict. Liminality, in Turner's own words with which this book has opened and with which it fairly has to end, is a 'cultural realm that has few or none of the attributes of the past or coming state' (Turner, 1969, p. 94), and liminars are 'neither here nor there; they are betwixt and between' (Turner, 1969, p. 95). Liminality is essentially a phase of transition between a familiar past and a future that can be partially foreseeable or unknown, although the transition can last long or even become permanent, as Turner himself (1974a, p. 261) anticipated when acknowledging the likelihood of 'a style of life that is permanently contained within liminality... Instead of the liminal being a passage, it seemed to be coming to be regarded as a state.'

The growing interest for liminality that has been recorded in a wide range of fields has allowed to expand on the knowledge of the core elements undergirding a liminal experience, which are a feeling of spacelessness and timelessness; the rites and ceremonies marking its inception, development, and end; the surfacing of an anti-structure; the birth and growth of a communitas among liminars, and the identity work that liminars engage in. Each of these elements has been specified in terms of the dimensions that the research on the topic has highlighted over the years. Maybe most remarkable is the relevance assumed by individual agency within a framework that has long emphasized the collective processes accompanying the suspension between a 'here' and 'there,' and a 'before' and an 'after.' Individuals' responses and reactions to being 'betwixt and between' disclose a way to cope with the uncertainty related to liminality through which potential drawbacks are reduced, while some benefits, or at least a peaceful forbearance of suspension, are pursued.

The dimensions that emerge from studies on liminality that are depicted in Figure 4.1 inform our understanding of liminality as a multi-faceted construct and can provide the inspiration for further research, be it qualitative or quantitative. It throws into sharp relief the necessity to adopt an emic perspective on liminality that grasps and emphasizes actors' perceptions and feelings rather than researchers' interpretations (Zabuski and Barley, 1997). The starting point to parse out liminality is that of realizing individuals' own articulation of their experience of being 'stuck in the middle' between the past and the future, suspended between a previous state or role and a looming one. Conversely, it has been underlined how the prevailing approach in empirical studies on this issue has embraced a

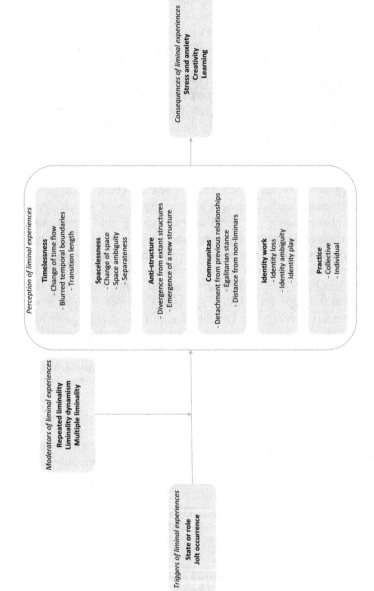

Figure 4.1 A model of liminal experiences.

stance in which liminality is attributed by virtue of being in a given state or having a given role—a consultant, an interorganizational network manager, a temporary worker.

The articulation of the liminal experience can be grasped through qualitative, but also quantitative research. The vast majority of the empirical research carried out so far is qualitative: most studies in the various fields examined are in fact based on semi-structured or open interviews (e.g., Sturdy et al., 2006; Swan et al., 2016; Bamber et al., 2017), some resort to archival documents (e.g., Tempest et al., 2007), and only a few rely on ethnographies (e.g., Richter, 2016). The elucidation of the dimensions of a liminal experience offered here paves the way for a systematic inquiry within the sphere of qualitative studies: the protocols for the interviews, e.g., could draw from the model shown in Figure 4.1, defining questions that target each of the dimensions included.

There is also a call for exploring liminality through quantitative studies (Ibarra and Obodaru, 2016). In particular, the lack of a scale able to gauge the liminal experience has been reported. The model accounted for in this chapter can represent the reference to build a scale: to achieve this goal, the single dimensions need to be expressed through ad hoc items. In the construction of the scale, the fundamental difference between Turner's theorization of liminality and subsequent contribution to the topic has to be kept in mind. Whereas, according to Turner, a liminal experience comprises all the core elements examined in Chapter 1 and depicted in the model (timelessness, spacelessness, rituals, anti-structure, communitas, identity work) and their joint presence is a proxy for a liminal phenomenon, reflection in other domains seems to suggest that not all the elements must be present in order for a social phenomenon to be interpreted as liminal or that they can change along the passage. Just to mention an example, timelessness, spacelessness, and a sense of communitas are the elements that, in Vesala and Tuomivaara's (2018) study, denote the liminality of the professionals participating in a week-long workshop in a remote location, while rituals, anti-structure, and identity work are not delved into. In the purest form offered by Turner, a scale targeting liminality would be reflective; that is, all the elements are interrelated, while in the latter, more recent stance assumed in different fields, the scale would be formative; that is, its elements are not expected to correlate (Bagozzi, 2011; Christophersen and Konradt, 2012). Elaboration and test of a scale will assist in overcoming this discrepancy.

Finally, in order for a process perspective to be developed based on the conceptualization originally provided in anthropology, the antecedents and the consequences of liminal experiences have to be integrated. Focusing on the antecedents, we know from the literature that a liminal experience may be triggered by some states or roles, such as working as a consultant, dealing with a disease, or being a traveler (Czarniawska and Mazza, 2003; Huang et al., 2018), or from unforeseen jolts, such as an incident that subverts ordinary life or the loss of a long-held job (Powley, 2009; O'Loughlin et al., 2017). It has to be once more reminded, though, that the embeddedness in a situation, the adoption of a role, or the occurrence of a jolt cannot identify liminality in a homogeneous way for all the individuals involves, as the growth of a liminality competence or 'muscle,' multiple types of liminality experienced simultaneously, and their likely evolving nature, analyzed in Chapter 3, influence the articulation of a liminal experience (e.g., Szakolczai, 2009; Adorno, 2015; Ibarra and Obodaru, 2016; Söderlund and Borg, 2018)). Concerning the aftermath, different liminal experiences can spawn different effects in terms of stress and anxiety (Garsten, 1999; Hawkins and Edwards, 2015), creativity (Howard-Grenville, Golden-Biddle, Irwin, and Mao, 2011; Bamber et al., 2017), and learning opportunities (Tempest and Starkey, 2004; Borg and Söderlund, 2015). A few relationships between the elements of the liminal experience and its outcomes can be posited by bringing together some inkling offered in this book. Liminars' ability to react through individual tactics against the suspension can reduce the negative impact of inhabiting a 'twilight zone,' releasing cognitive and behavioral resources for delineating new courses of action. In a related vein, being nested in a network of egalitarian and supportive ties with peers can increase resilience in the wake of uncertainty, reducing the feeling of unease and anxiety.

In conclusion, liminality is a truly transdisciplinary concept that has been attracting the effort and the passion of scholars in a variety of fields. Organizational researchers have mostly focused on short- or long-term transitions faced by consultants and by contingent workers through their engagement in projects, but also by teams affected by unexpected events, and by hybrid entrepreneurs and multiple careerists. Health studies have seen liminality as a situation potentially applicable to individuals who deal with a disability, a chronic, or a life-threatening disease. But liminality has also been a relevant issue in sociology when framing the experiences of migrants and prisoners, for instance. In a yet different domain, liminality has been at the core of reflection on tourism and education, in which travels, on one side, and university programs, on the other, represent a suspension between what is left behind and what may loom ahead. All the speculation and empirical investigations have proceeded along parallel tracks, without reciprocally exploiting the stimulating hints provided by other lines of inquiry. Time is ripe to join forces and move towards a comprehension of the experience of being 'betwixt and between' that, as the model construed in this book intends to do, integrates and benefits from the research that scholars, regardless of their domain of expertise, have rigorously and fervently devoted to liminality.

References

Adorno, G. (2015). Between two worlds: Liminality and late-stage cancer-directed therapy. *OMEGA-Journal of Death and Dying, 71*(2), 99–125.

Ahrne, G. (1994). *Social organizations: Interaction inside, outside and between organizations.* London, UK: Sage.

Alboher, M. (2007). *One person multiple careers.* New York: Warner Books.

Alighieri, D. (2017). *The divine comedy.* Aegitas Digital Publi.

Arthur, M. B. (2008). Examining contemporary careers: A call for interdisciplinary inquiry. *Human Relations, 61*(2), 163–186.

Arthur, M. B., Khapova, S. N., & Wilderom, C. P. (2005). Career success in a boundaryless career world. *Journal of Organizational Behavior, 26*(2), 177–202.

Ashford, S. J., George, E., & Blatt, R. (2007). 2 old assumptions, new work: The opportunities and challenges of research on nonstandard employment. *The Academy of Management Annals, 1*(1), 65–117.

Ashforth, B. E., Kreiner, G. E., & Fugate, M. (2000). All in a day's work: Boundaries and micro role transitions. *Academy of Management Review, 25*(3), 472–491.

Ashforth, B. E., & Tomiuk, M. A. (2000). Emotional labour and authenticity: Views from service agents. In S. Fineman (Ed.), *Emotion in organizations* (2nd ed., pp. 184–203). London, UK: Sage.

Atkinson, S., & Robson, M. (2012). Arts and health as a practice of liminality: Managing the spaces of transformation for social and emotional wellbeing with primary school children. *Health & Place, 18*(6), 1348–1355.

Averett, S. L. (2001). Moonlighting: Multiple motives and gender differences. *Applied Economics, 33*(11), 1391–1410.

Bagozzi, R. P. (2011). Measurement and meaning in information systems and organizational research: Methodological and philosophical foundations. *MIS Quarterly, 35*, 261–292.

Bamber, M., Allen-Collinson, J., & McCormack, J. (2017). Occupational limbo, transitional liminality and permanent liminality: New conceptual distinctions. *Human Relations, 70*(12), 1514–1537.

Barley, S. R., Bechky, B. A., & Milliken, F. J. (2017). The changing nature of work: Careers, identities, and work lives in the 21st century. *Academy of Management Discoveries, 3*, 111–115.

Barley, S. R., & Kunda, G. (2001). Bringing work back in. *Organization Science, 12*(1), 76–95.

Barley, S. R., & Kunda, G. (2004). *Gurus, hired guns, and warm bodies: Itinerant experts in a knowledge economy.* Princeton, NJ: Princeton University Press.

Bechky, B. A. (2003). Sharing meaning across occupational communities: The transformation of understanding on a production floor. *Organization Science, 14*(3), 312–330.

Beech, N. (2008). On the nature of dialogic identity work. *Organization, 15*(1), 51–74.

Beech, N. (2011). Liminality and the practices of identity reconstruction. *Human Relations, 64*(2), 285–302.

Bidwell, M., Briscoe, F., Fernandez-Mateo, I., & Sterling, A. (2013). The employment relationship and inequality: How and why changes in employment practices are reshaping rewards in organizations. *Academy of Management Annals, 7*(1), 61–121.

Bigger, S. (2009). Victor Turner, liminality, and cultural performance. *Journal of Beliefs & Values, 30*(2), 209–212.

Blank, R. (1998), Contingent work in a changing labor market. In R. Freeman & P. Gottschalk (Eds.), *Generating jobs: How to increase demand for less-skilled workers* (pp. 258–294). New York, NY: Russell Sage.

Blows, E., Bird, L., Seymour, J., & Cox, K. (2012). Liminality as a framework for understanding the experience of cancer survivorship: A literature review. *Journal of Advanced Nursing, 68*(10), 2155–2164.

Boland, T. (2013). Towards an anthropology of critique: The modern experience of liminality and crisis. *Anthropological Theory, 13*(3), 222–239.

Borg, E., & Söderlund, J. (2013). Moving in, moving on: Liminality practices in project-based work. *Employee Relations, 36*(2), 182–197.

Borg, E., & Söderlund, J. (2015). Liminality competence: An interpretative study of mobile project workers' conception of liminality at work. *Management Learning, 46*(3), 260–279.

Brown, A. D. (2015). Identities and identity work in organizations. *International Journal of Management Reviews, 17*(1), 20–40.

Brown, B., Huszar, K., & Chapman, R. (2017). 'Betwixt and between'; liminality in recovery stories from people with myalgic encephalomyelitis (ME) or chronic fatigue syndrome (CFS). *Sociology of Health & Illness, 39*(5), 696–710.

Bui, H. T., Wilkins, H., & Lee, Y. S. (2014). Liminal experience of East Asian backpackers. *Tourist Studies, 14*(2), 126–143.

Burke, P. J., & Stets, J. E. (2009). *Identity theory.* New York, NY: Oxford University Press.

Campbell, J. (1972). *Myths to live by.* London, UK: Penguin.

Cappelli, P., & Keller, J. R. (2013). Classifying work in the new economy. *Academy of Management Review, 38*(4), 575–596.

Caza, B. B., Moss, S., & Vough, H. (2017). From synchronizing to harmonizing: The process of authenticating multiple work identities. *Administrative Science Quarterly*, doi: 10.1177/0001839217733972

Caza, B. B., Vough, H., & Puranik, H. (2018). Identity work in organizations and occupations: Definitions, theories, and pathways forward. *Journal of Organizational Behavior, 39*(7), 889–910.

Charmaz, K., & Belgrave, L. L. (2013). Modern symbolic interaction theory and health. In W. C. Cockerham (Ed.), *Medical sociology on the move* (pp. 11–39). Dordrecht, The Netherlands: Springer.

Christianson, M. K., Farkas, M. T., Sutcliffe, K. M., & Weick, K. E. (2009). Learning through rare events: Significant interruptions at the Baltimore & Ohio Railroad Museum. *Organization Science, 20*(5), 846–860.

Clegg, S., Pina e Cunha, M., Rego, A., & Story, J. (2015). Powers of romance: The liminal challenges of managing organizational intimacy. *Journal of Management Inquiry, 24*(2), 131–148.

Clegg, S. R., Kornberger, M., & Rhodes, C. (2004). Noise, parasites and translation: Theory and practice in management consulting. *Management Learning, 35*(1), 31–44.

Cody, K., & Lawlor, K. (2011). On the borderline: Exploring liminal consumption and the negotiation of threshold selves. *Marketing Theory, 11*(2), 207–228.

Cohen, A. (2002). *The perfect store. Inside eBay.* New York, NY: Little, Brown and Company.

Cohen, S. A. (2011). Lifestyle travellers: Backpacking as a way of life. *Annals of Tourism Research, 38*(4), 1535–1555.

Cohen, S. G., & Bailey, D. E. (1997). What makes teams work: Group effectiveness research from the shop floor to the executive suite. *Journal of management, 23*(3), 239–290.

Cohn, E. S. (2001). From waiting to relating: Parents' experiences in the waiting room of an occupational therapy clinic. *American Journal of Occupational Therapy, 55*(2), 167–174.

Comfort, M. L. (2003). In the tube at San Quentin: The "secondary prisonization" of women visiting inmates. *Journal of Contemporary Ethnography, 32*(1), 77–107.

Concannon, M., & Nordberg, D. (2018). Boards strategizing in liminal spaces: Process and practice, formal and informal. *European Management Journal, 36*(1), 71–82.

Connelly, C. E., & Gallagher, D. G. (2004). Emerging trends in contingent work research. *Journal of management, 30*(6), 959–983.

Conroy, S. A., & O'Leary-Kelly, A. M. (2014). Letting go and moving on: Work-related identity loss and recovery. *Academy of Management Review, 39*(1), 67–87.

Conway, K. S., & Kimmel, J. (1998). Male labor supply estimates and the decision to moonlight. *Labour Economics, 5*(2), 135–166.

Cook-Sather, A. (2006). Newly betwixt and between: Revising liminality in the context of a teacher preparation program. *Anthropology & Education Quarterly, 37*(2), 110–127.

Corley, K. G., & Gioia, D. A. (2004). Identity ambiguity and change in the wake of a corporate spin-off. *Administrative Science Quarterly, 49*(2), 173–208.

Christophersen, T., & Konradt, U. (2012). Development and validation of a formative and a reflective measure for the assessment of online store usability. *Behaviour & Information Technology, 31*(9), 839–857.

Cronin, C., Ryrie, A., Huntley, T., & Hayton, J. (2018). 'Sinking and swimming in disability coaching': An autoethnographic account of coaching in a new context. *Qualitative Research in Sport, Exercise and Health, 10*(3), 362–377.

Czarniawska, B., & Mazza, C. (2003). Consulting as a liminal space. *Human Relations, 56*(3), 267–290.

Czarniawska, B., & Mazza, C. (2012). Consultants and clients from constructivist perspectives. In T. Clark & M. Kipping (Eds.), *The Oxford handbook of management consulting* (pp. 427–445). Oxford, UK: Oxford University Press.

Czarniawska-Joerges, B. (1990). Merchants of meaning: Management consulting in the Swedish public sector. In B. A. Turner (Ed.), *Organizational symbolism* (pp. 139–150). Berlin, Boston: de Gruyter.

Dale, K., & Burrell, G. (2008). *The spaces of organisation and the organisation of space: Power, identity and materiality at work.* Basingstoke: Palgrave Macmillan.

Daniel, E., & Ellis-Chadwick, F. (2016). Entrepreneurship and liminality: The case of self-storage based businesses. *International Journal of Entrepreneurial Behavior & Research, 22*(3), 436–457.

Daskalaki, M., & Simosi, M. (2018). Unemployment as a liminoid phenomenon: Identity trajectories in times of crisis. *Human Relations, 71*(9), 1153–1178.

Davis-Blake, A., & Uzzi, B. (1993). Determinants of employment externalization: A study of temporary workers and independent contractors. *Administrative Science Quarterly, 38*(2), 195–223.

Delanty, G. (2010). *Community* (2nd ed.). Abingdon: Routledge.

Del Vecchio Good, M. J., Good, B. J., Schaffer, C., & Lind, S. E. (1990). American oncology and the discourse on hope. *Culture, Medicine and Psychiatry, 14*(1), 59–79.

Demetry, D. (2017). Pop-up to professional: Emerging entrepreneurial identity and evolving vocabularies of motive. *Academy of Management Discoveries, 3*(2), 187–207.

De Stefano, V. (2016). The rise of the "just-in time workforce": On demand work, crowdwork, and labor protection in the "gig economy". *Comparative Labor Law and Policy Journal, 37*(3), 461–471.

Di Domenico, M., Daniel, E., & Nunan, D. (2014). 'Mental mobility' in the digital age: Entrepreneurs and the online home-based business. *New Technology, Work and Employment, 29*(3), 266–281.

Douglas, M. (1966). *Purity and danger: An analysis of concepts of pollution and taboo*. London, UK: Routledge & Kegan Paul.

Dubouloy, M. (2004). The transitional space and self-recovery: A psychoanalytical approach to high-potential managers' training. *Human Relations, 57*(4), 467–496.

Dukerich, J. M., Golden, B. R., & Shortell, S. M. (2002). Beauty is in the eye of the beholder: The impact of organizational identification, identity, and image on the cooperative behaviors of physicians. *Administrative Science Quarterly, 47*(3), 507–533.

Dutton, J. E., Dukerich, J. M., & Harquail, C. V. (1994). Organizational images and member identification. *Administrative Science Quarterly, 39*(2), 239–263.

Ebaugh, H. R., & Ebaugh, H. R. F. (1988). *Becoming an ex: The process of role exit*. Chicago, IL: University of Chicago Press.

Edwards, G. (2011). Concepts of community: A framework for contextualizing distributed leadership. *International Journal of Management Reviews, 13*(3), 301–312.

Ellis, N., & Ybema, S. (2010). Marketing identities: Shifting circles of identification in inter-organizational relationships. *Organization Studies, 31*(3), 279–305.

Eriksson-Zetterquist, U. (2002). Gender construction in corporations. In B. Czarniawska & H. Höpfl (Eds.), *Casting the other: Production and maintenance of inequality in organizations* (pp. 89–103). London, UK: Routledge.

Fauchart, E., & Gruber, M. (2011). Darwinians, communitarians, and missionaries: The role of founder identity in entrepreneurship. *Academy of Management Journal, 54*(5), 935–957.

Fisher, S. L., & Connelly, C. E. (2017). Lower cost or just lower value? Modeling the organizational costs and benefits of contingent work. *Academy of Management Discoveries, 3*(2), 165–186.

Fogarty, H., Scott, P., & Williams, S. (2011). The half-empty office: Dilemmas in managing locational flexibility. *New Technology, Work and Employment, 26*(3), 183–195.

Folta, T. B., Delmar, F., & Wennberg, K. (2010). Hybrid entrepreneurship. *Management Science, 56*(2), 253–269.

Galagan, P. (2013). What's your gig? *T + D, 67*(3), 26–28.

Galperin, R. V. (2017). Mass-production of professional services and pseudo-professional identity in tax preparation work. *Academy of Management Discoveries, 3*(2), 208–229.

Garcia-Lorenzo, L., Donnelly, P., Sell-Trujillo, L., & Imas, J. M. (2018). Liminal entrepreneuring: The creative practices of nascent necessity entrepreneurs. *Organization Studies, 39*(2–3), 373–395.

Garsten, C. (1999). Betwixt and between: Temporary employees as liminal subjects in flexible organizations. *Organization Studies, 20*(4), 601–617.

George, E., & Chattopadhyay, P. (2005). One foot in each camp: The dual identification of contract workers. *Administrative Science Quarterly, 50*(1), 68–99.

Goodman, N. (1978). *Ways of worldmaking.* Indianapolis, IN: Hackett Publishers.

Goss, D., & Bridson, J. (1998). Understanding interim management. *Human Resource Management Journal, 8*(4), 37–50.

Grant, R. M. (1996). Toward a knowledge-based theory of the firm. *Strategic Management Journal, 17*(S2), 109–122.

Grue, J. (2014). Technically disabled, ill for all practical purposes? Myalgic encephalopathy/chronic fatigue syndrome discourse in Norway. *Disability & Society, 29*(2), 213–223.

Hackman, J. R., & Wageman, R. (2005). A theory of team coaching. *Academy of Management Review, 30*(2), 269–287.

Hall, J. V., & Krueger, A. B. (2018). An analysis of the labor market for Uber's driver-partners in the United States. *ILR Review, 71*(3), 705–732.

Hallier, J., & James, P. (1999). Group rites and trainer wrongs in employee experiences of job change. *Journal of Management Studies, 36*(1), 45–67.

Harley, B. (1999). The myth of empowerment: work organisation, hierarchy and employee autonomy in contemporary Australian workplaces. *Work, Employment and Society, 13*(1), 41–66.

Haski-Leventhal, D., & Bargal, D. (2008). The volunteer stages and transitions model: Organizational socialization of volunteers. *Human Relations, 61*(1), 67–102.

Hawkins, B., & Edwards, G. (2015). Managing the monsters of doubt: Liminality, threshold concepts and leadership learning. *Management Learning, 46*(1), 24–43.

Henfridsson, O., & Yoo, Y. (2013). The liminality of trajectory shifts in institutional entrepreneurship. *Organization Science, 25*(3), 932–950.

Hewlin, P. F., Dumas, T. L., & Burnett, M. F. (2017). To thine own self be true? Facades of conformity, values incongruence, and the moderating impact of leader integrity. *Academy of Management Journal, 60*(1), 178–199.

Hipple, S. F. (2010). Multiple jobholding during the 2000s. *Monthly Labor Review, 133*(7), 21–32.

Hodgson, D. E., & Paton, S. (2016). Understanding the professional project manager: Cosmopolitans, locals and identity work. *International Journal of Project Management, 34*(2), 352–364.

Hoel Felde, L. K. (2011). 'I take a small amount of the real product': Elevated cholesterol and everyday medical reasoning in liminal space. *Health, 15*(6), 604–619.

Horvath, A., Thomassen, B., & Wydra, H. (Eds.). (2015). *Breaking boundaries: Varieties of liminality.* New York, Oxford: Berghahn Books.

Howard-Grenville, J., Golden-Biddle, K., Irwin, J., & Mao, J. (2011). Liminality as cultural process for cultural change. *Organization Science, 22*(2), 522–539.

Hoyer, P., & Steyaert, C. (2015). Narrative identity construction in times of career change: Taking note of unconscious desires. *Human Relations, 68*(12), 1837–1863.

Huang, W. J., Xiao, H., & Wang, S. (2018). Airports as liminal space. *Annals of Tourism Research, 70*, 1–13.

Huyghe, A., Knockaert, M., & Obschonka, M. (2016). Unraveling the "passion orchestra" in academia. *Journal of Business Venturing, 31*(3), 344–364.

Ibarra, H. (1999). Provisional selves: Experimenting with image and identity in professional adaptation. *Administrative Science Quarterly, 44*(4), 764–791.

Ibarra, H. (2004). *Working identity: Unconventional strategies for reinventing your career.* Boston, MA: Harvard Business Press.

Ibarra, H., & Barbulescu, R. (2010). Identity as narrative: Prevalence, effectiveness, and consequences of narrative identity work in macro work role transitions. *Academy of Management Review, 35*(1), 135–154.

Ibarra, H., & Obodaru, O. (2016). Betwixt and between identities: Liminal experience in contemporary careers. *Research in Organizational Behavior, 36*, 47–64.

Ibarra, H., & Petriglieri, J. L. (2010). Identity work and play. *Journal of Organizational Change Management, 23*(1), 10–25.

Ibarra, H., Snook, S., & Guillen Ramo, L. (2010). Identity-based leader development. In N. Nohria & R. Khurana (Eds.), *Handbook of leadership theory and practice* (pp. 657–678). Boston, MA: Harvard Business Press.

Iedema, R., Degeling, P., Braithwaite, J., & White, L. (2004). 'It's an interesting conversation I'm hearing': The doctor as manager. *Organization Studies, 25*(1), 15–33.

Inkson, K., Heising, A., & Rousseau, D. M. (2001). The Interim manager: Prototype of the 21st-century worker? *Human Relations, 54*(3), 259–284.

Jahn, S., Cornwell, T. B., Drengner, J., & Gaus, H. (2018). Temporary communitas and willingness to return to events. *Journal of Business Research, 92*, 329–338.

Jain, S., George, G., & Maltarich, M. (2009). Academics or entrepreneurs? Investigating role identity modification of university scientists involved in commercialization activity. *Research Policy, 38*(6), 922–935.

Jones, C., & Spicer, A. (2005). The sublime object of entrepreneurship. *Organization, 12*(2), 223–246.

Jones, C., & Spicer, A. (2009). *Unmasking the entrepreneur.* Cheltenham, UK: Edward Elgar.

Johnsen, C. G., & Sørensen, B. M. (2015). 'It's capitalism on coke!': From temporary to permanent liminality in organization studies. *Culture and Organization, 21*(4), 321–337.

Jordhus-Lier, D., Underthun, A., & Zampoukos, K. (2017). Changing workplace geographies: Restructuring warehouse employment in the Oslo region. *Environment and Planning A: Economy and Space, 51*(1), 69–90.

Joy, F. (2009). *Hybrid entrepreneurship: How the middle class can beat the slow economy, earn extra income and reclaim the American dream.* Atlanta, GA: Joy Group Press.

Kayes, D. (2006). *Destructive goal pursuit: The Mt. Everest disaster.* New York, NY: Palgrave Macmillan.

Kalleberg, A. L. (2001). Organizing flexibility: The flexible firm in a new century. *British Journal of Industrial Relations, 39*(4), 479–504.

Kalleberg, A. L. (2003). Flexible firms and labor market segmentation: Effects of workplace restructuring on jobs and workers. *Work and Occupations, 30*(2), 154–175.

Karhunen, P., Olimpieva, I., & Hytti, U. (2017). Identity work of science-based entrepreneurs in Finland and in Russia. *Entrepreneurship & Regional Development, 29*(5–6), 544–566.

Karioris, F. G. (2016). Temporally adrift and permanently liminal: Relations, distalgia and a US University as site of transition and frontier. *Culture Unbound: Journal of Current Cultural Research, 8*(1), 88–103.

Katz, L. F., & Krueger, A. B. (2016). *The rise and nature of alternative work arrangements in the United States, 1995–2015* (No. w22667). National Bureau of Economic Research.

Kellerman, A. (2008). International airports: Passengers in an environment of "authorities". *Mobilities, 3*(1), 161–178.

Kenney, M., & Zysman, J. (2016). The rise of the platform economy. *Issues in Science and Technology, 32*(3), 61.

Kirk, K., Bal, E., & Janssen, S. R. (2017). Migrants in liminal time and space: An exploration of the experiences of highly skilled Indian bachelors in Amsterdam. *Journal of Ethnic and Migration Studies, 43*(16), 2771–2787.

Klein, A., & Williams, L. (2012). Immigration detention in the community: Research on the experiences of migrants released from detention centres in the UK. *Population, Space and Place, 18*(6), 741–753.

Kociatkiewicz, J., & Kostera, M. (2011). Transitional space. *Tamara: Journal for Critical Organization Inquiry, 9*(3–4), 7–9.

Kornberger, M., Justesen, L., & Mouritsen, J. (2011). "When you make manager, we put a big mountain in front of you": An ethnography of managers in a Big 4 accounting firm. *Accounting, Organizations and Society, 36*(8), 514–533.

Krishnan, P. (1990). The economics of moonlighting: A double self-selection model. *The Review of Economics and Statistics, 72*(2), 361–367.

Krueger Jr, N. F., Reilly, M. D., & Carsrud, A. L. (2000). Competing models of entrepreneurial intentions. *Journal of Business Venturing, 15*(5–6), 411–432.

Kunda, G. (1992). *Engineering culture.* Philadelphia, PA: Temple University Press.

Kunda, G., Barley, S. R., & Evans, J. (2002). Why do contractors contract? The experience of highly skilled technical professionals in a contingent labor market. *ILR Review, 55*(2), 234–261.

Küpers, W. (2011). Dancing on the līmen. Embodied and creative inter-places as thresholds of be (com)ing: Phenomenological perspectives on liminality and transitional spaces in organisation and leadership. *Tamara: Journal for Critical Organization Inquiry, 9*(3–4), 45–59.

Ladge, J. J., Clair, J. A., & Greenberg, D. (2012). Cross-domain identity transition during liminal periods: Constructing multiple selves as professional and mother during pregnancy. *Academy of Management Journal, 55*(6), 1449–1471.

Lalé, E. (2015). Multiple jobholding over the past two decades. *Monthly Labour Review, 138*, 1.

Land, R., Rattray, J., & Vivian, P. (2014). Learning in the liminal space: A semiotic approach to threshold concepts. *Higher Education, 67*(2), 199–217.

Lindkvist, L. (2005). Knowledge communities and knowledge collectivities: A typology of knowledge work in groups. *Journal of Management Studies, 42*(6), 1189–1210.

Little, M., Jordens, C. F., Paul, K., Montgomery, K., & Philipson, B. (1998). Liminality: A major category of the experience of cancer illness. *Social Science & Medicine, 47*(10), 1485–1494.

Louis, M. R. (1980). Career transitions: Varieties and commonalities. *Academy of Management Review, 5*(3), 329–340.

Louis, M. R. (1982). Managing career transition: A missing link in career development. *Organizational Dynamics, 10*(4), 68–77.

Luhmann, N. (2005). Communication barriers in management consulting. In D. Seidl & K. H. Becker (Eds.), *Niklas Luhmann and organization studies* (pp. 351–364). Copenhagen: Copenhagen Business School Press.

Manigart, S., Wright, M., Robbie, K., Desbrieres, P., & De Waele, K. (1997). Venture capitalists' appraisal of investment projects: An empirical European study. *Entrepreneurship Theory and Practice, 21*(4), 29–43.

Manyika, J., Lund, S., Bughin, J., Robinson, K., Mischke, J., & Mahajan, D. (2016). *Independent work: Choice, necessity, and the gig economy.* Washington, DC: McKinsey Global Institute.

Marchington, M., Grimshaw, D., Rubery, J., & Willmott, H. (2005). *Fragmenting work: Blurring organizational boundaries and disordering hierarchies.* Oxford, UK: Oxford University Press.

Marchington, M., & Vincent, S. (2004). Analysing the influence of institutional, organizational and interpersonal forces in shaping inter-organizational relations. *Journal of Management Studies, 41*(6), 1029–1056.

Markus, H., & Nurius, P. (1986). Possible selves. *American Psychologist, 41*(9), 954–969.

Mattarelli, E., Tagliaventi, M. R., Carli, G., & Gupta, A. (2017). The role of brokers and social identities in the development of capabilities in global virtual teams. *Journal of International Management, 23*(4), 382–398.

McClement, S. E., & Woodgate, R. L. (1997). Care of the terminally ill cachectic cancer patient: Interface between nursing and psychological anthropology. *European Journal of Cancer Care, 6*(4), 295–303.

McGinnis, P. J. (2016). *The 10% entrepreneur: Live your startup dream without quitting your day job.* New York, NY: Penguin.

Mayrhofer, W., & Iellatchitch, A. (2005). Rites, right? The value of rites de passage for dealing with today's career transitions. *Career Development International, 10*(1), 52–66.

McKinsey & Co. (2016). *Independent work: Choice, necessity, and the gig economy*. New York, NY: McKinsey Global Institute.

Mohe, M., & Seidl, D. (2011). Theorizing the client—consultant relationship from the perspective of social-systems theory. *Organization, 18*(1), 3–22.

Moran, D. (2013). Between outside and inside? Prison visiting rooms as liminal carceral spaces. *GeoJournal, 78*(2), 339–351.

Murphy, R. (1987). *The body silent: A journey into paralysis.* New York, NY: Henry Holt.

Murphy, R. (1995). Encounters: The body silent in America. In B. Ingstad & S. R. Whyte (Eds.), *Disability and culture* (pp. 140–158). Berkely, Los Angeles, London: University of California Press.

Murphy, R. F., Scheer, J., Murphy, Y., & Mack, R. (1988). Physical disability and social liminality: A study in the rituals of adversity. *Social Science & Medicine, 26*(2), 235–242.

Murray, F. (2010). The oncomouse that roared: Hybrid exchange strategies as a source of distinction at the boundary of overlapping institutions. *American Journal of Sociology, 116*(2), 341–388.

Navis, C., & Glynn, M. A. (2011). Legitimate distinctiveness and the entrepreneurial identity: Influence on investor judgments of new venture plausibility. *Academy of Management Review, 36*(3), 479–499.

Nguyen, A. M. D., & Benet-Martínez, V. (2013). Biculturalism and adjustment: A meta-analysis. *Journal of Cross-Cultural Psychology, 44*(1), 122–159.

Nippert-Eng, C. E. (1996). Calendars and keys: The classification of "home" and "work". *Sociological forum, 11*(3), 563–582.

Nippert-Eng, C. E. (2008). *Home and work: Negotiating boundaries through everyday life.* Chicago, IL: University of Chicago Press.

Noy, C., & Cohen, E. (2005). Introduction: Backpacking as a rite of passage in Israel. In C. Noy & E. Cohen (Eds.), *Israel backpackers and their society: A view from afar* (pp. 1–43). Albany, NY: State University of New York.

Obodaru, O. (2012). The self not taken: How alternative selves develop and how they influence our professional lives. *Academy of Management Review, 37*(1), 34–57.

O'Loughlin, D. M., Szmigin, I., McEachern, M. G., Barbosa, B., Karantinou, K., & Fernández-Moya, M. E. (2017). Man thou art dust: Rites of passage in austere times. *Sociology, 51*(5), 1050–1066.

Pace, M., & Pallister-Wilkins, P. (2018). EU–Hamas actors in a state of permanent liminality. *Journal of International Relations and Development, 21*(1), 223–246.

Paxson, C. H., & Sicherman, N. (1996). The dynamics of dual job holding and job mobility. *Journal of Labor Economics, 14*(3), 357–393.

Pedulla, D. S. (2013). The hidden costs of contingency: Employers' use of contingent workers and standard employees' outcomes. *Social Forces, 92*(2), 691–722.

Petriglieri, G., Ashford, S. J., & Wrzesniewski, A. (2019). Agony and ecstasy in the gig economy: Cultivating holding environments for precarious and personalized work identities. *Administrative Science Quarterly, 64*(1), 124–170.

Petriglieri, G., & Petriglieri, J. L. (2010). Identity workspaces: The case of business schools. *Academy of Management Learning & Education, 9*(1), 44–60.

Petriglieri, G., Petriglieri J. L., & Wood, J. D. (2018). Fast tracks and inner journeys: Crafting portable selves for contemporary careers. *Administrative Science Quarterly, 63*(3), 479–525.

Petriglieri, J. L. (2011). Under threat: Responses to and the consequences of threats to individuals' identities. *Academy of Management Review, 36*(4), 641–662.

Petrova, K. (2012). Part-time entrepreneurship and financial constraints: Evidence from the panel study of entrepreneurial dynamics. *Small Business Economics, 39*(2), 473–493.

Phillips, M. J. (1990). Damaged goods: Oral narratives of the experience of disability in American culture. *Social Science & Medicine, 30*(8), 849–857.

Pina e Cunha, M. P., Guimarães-Costa, N., Rego, A., & Clegg, S. R. (2010). Leading and following (un)ethically in Limen. *Journal of Business Ethics, 97*(2), 189–206.

Powley, E. H. (2009). Reclaiming resilience and safety: Resilience activation in the critical period of crisis. *Human Relations, 62*(9), 1289–1326.

Pratt, M. G., Rockmann, K. W., & Kaufmann, J. B. (2006). Constructing professional identity: The role of work and identity learning cycles in the customization of identity among medical residents. *Academy of Management Journal, 49*(2), 235–262.

Pritchard, A., & Morgan, N. (2006). Hotel Babylon? Exploring hotels as liminal sites of transition and transgression. *Tourism Management, 27*(5), 762–772.

Raab, J., & Kenis, P. (2009). Heading toward a society of networks: Empirical developments and theoretical challenges. *Journal of Management Inquiry, 18*(3), 198–210.

Raffiee, J., & Feng, J. (2014). Should I quit my day job? A hybrid path to entrepreneurship. *Academy of Management Journal, 57*(4), 936–963.

Ramarajan, L., Rothbard, N. P., & Wilk, S. L. (2017). Discordant vs. harmonious selves: The effects of identity conflict and enhancement on sales performance in employee–customer interactions. *Academy of Management Journal, 60*(6), 2208–2238.

Reid-Cunningham, A. R. (2009). Anthropological theories of disability. *Journal of Human Behavior in the Social Environment, 19*(1), 99–111.

Reilly, P. (2017). The layers of a clown: Career development in cultural production industries. *Academy of Management Discoveries, 3*(2), 145–164.

Richter, L. (2016). On the edge of existence: Malian migrants in the Maghreb. *Culture Unbound: Journal of Current Cultural Research, 8*(1), 74–87.

Ryan, A. (2019). Guiding and enabling liminal experiences between business and arts organizations operating in a sponsorship relationship. *Human Relations, 72*(2), 344–369.

Sankowska, A., & Söderlund, J. (2015). Trust, reflexivity and knowledge integration: Toward a conceptual framework concerning mobile engineers. *Human Relations, 68*(6), 973–1000.

Schulz, M. (2018). *Hybrid entrepreneurship*. BoD–Books on Demand.

Schulz, M., Urbig, D., & Procher, V. (2016). Hybrid entrepreneurship and public policy: The case of firm entry deregulation. *Journal of Business Venturing, 31*(3), 272–286.

Sharpley, R., & Sundaram, P. (2005). Tourism: A sacred journey? The case of ashram tourism, India. *International Journal of Tourism Research, 7*(3), 161–171.

Shishko, R., & Rostker, B. (1976). The economics of multiple job holding. *The American Economic Review, 66*(3), 298–308.

Shortt, H. (2015). Liminality, space and the importance of 'transitory dwelling places' at work. *Human Relations, 68*(4), 633–658.

Sleight, A. G. (2016). Liminality and ritual in biographical work: A theoretical framework for cancer survivorship. *International Journal of Transpersonal Studies, 35*(1), 52–61.

Sliter, M. T., & Boyd, E. M. (2014). Two (or three) is not equal to one: Multiple jobholding as a neglected topic in organizational research. *Journal of Organizational Behavior, 35*(7), 1042–1046.

Snow, D. A., & Anderson, L. (1987). Identity work among the homeless: The verbal construction and avowal of personal identities. *American Journal of Sociology, 92*(6), 1336–1371.

Söderlund, J. (2004). Building theories of project management: Past research, questions for the future. *International Journal of Project Management, 22*(3), 183–191.

Söderlund, J., & Borg, E. (2018). Liminality in management and organization studies: Process, position and place. *International Journal of Management Reviews, 20*(4), 880–902.

Solesvik, M. Z. (2017). Hybrid entrepreneurship: How and why entrepreneurs combine employment with self-employment. *Technology Innovation Management Review, 7*(3), 33–41.

Stryker, S., & Burke, P. J. (2000). The past, present, and future of an identity theory. *Social Psychology Quarterly, 63*(4), 284–297.

Sturdy, A. (2011). Consultancy's consequences? A critical assessment of management consultancy's impact on management. *British Journal of Management, 22*(3), 517–530.

Sturdy, A., Handley, K., Clark, T., & Fincham, R. (2009). *Management consultancy: Boundaries and knowledge in action*. Oxford, UK: Oxford University Press on Demand.

Sturdy, A., Schwarz, M., & Spicer, A. (2006). Guess who's coming to dinner? Structures and uses of liminality in strategic management consultancy. *Human Relations, 59*(7), 929–960.

Sturdy, A., & Wright, C. (2011). The active client: The boundary-spanning roles of internal consultants as gatekeepers, brokers and partners of their external counterparts. *Management Learning, 42*(5), 485–503.

Sutton-Smith, B. (1972, December). Games of order and disorder. In *Symposium "Forms of Symbolic Inversion" at the American anthropological association, Toronto*, 17–19.

Sveningsson, S., & Alvesson, M. (2003). Managing managerial identities: Organizational fragmentation, discourse and identity struggle. *Human Relations, 56*(10), 1163–1193.

Swan, J., Scarbrough, H., & Ziebro, M. (2016). Liminal roles as a source of creative agency in management: The case of knowledge-sharing communities. *Human Relations, 69*(3), 781–811.

Swann Jr, W. B., Johnson, R. E., & Bosson, J. K. (2009). Identity negotiation at work. *Research in Organizational Behavior, 29*, 81–109.

Szakolczai, A. (2000). *Reflexive historical sociology*. New York, NY: Routledge.

Szakolczai, A. (2009). Liminality and experience: Structuring transitory situations and transformative events. *International Political Anthropology, 2*(1), 141–172.

Tansley, C., & Tietze, S. (2013). Rites of passage through talent management progression stages: An identity work perspective. *The International Journal of Human Resource Management, 24*(9), 1799–1815.

Tempest, S., & Starkey, K. (2004). The effects of liminality on individual and organizational learning. *Organization Studies, 25*(4), 507–527.

Tempest, S., Starkey, K., & Ennew, C. (2007). In the death zone: A study of limits in the 1996 Mount Everest disaster. *Human Relations, 60*(7), 1039–1064.

Teo, W. L., Lee, M., & Lim, W. S. (2017). The relational activation of resilience model: How leadership activates resilience in an organizational crisis. *Journal of Contingencies and Crisis Management, 25*(3), 136–147.

Thomassen, B. (2009). The uses and meanings of liminality. *International Political Anthropology, 2*(1), 5–27.

Thomassen, B. (2012). Notes towards an anthropology of political revolutions. *Comparative Studies in Society and History, 54*(3), 679–706.

Thomassen, B. (2014). *Liminality and the modern: Living through the in-between*. Farnham, UK: Routledge.

Thomassen, B. (2015). Thinking with liminality. In A. Horvath, B. Thomassen, & H. Wydra, (Eds.), *Breaking boundaries: Varieties of liminality* (pp. 39–58). New York, NY: Berghahn Books.

Thompson, K. (2007). Liminality as a descriptor for the cancer experience. *Illness, Crisis & Loss, 15*(4), 333–351.

Thorgren, S., Nordström, C., & Wincent, J. (2014). Hybrid entrepreneurship: The importance of passion. *Baltic Journal of Management, 9*(3), 314–329.

Thorgren, S., Sirén, C., Nordström, C., & Wincent, J. (2016). Hybrid entrepreneurs' second-step choice: The nonlinear relationship between age and intention to enter full-time entrepreneurship. *Journal of Business Venturing Insights, 5*, 14–18.

Thurlow, A., & Helms Mills, J. (2009). Change, talk and sensemaking. *Journal of Organizational Change Management, 22*(5), 459–479.

Turner, V. (1967). *The forest of symbols. Aspects of Ndembu ritual.* Ithaca, NY: Cornell University Press.

Turner, V. (1969). *The ritual process. Structure and anti-structure.* Ithaca, NY: Cornell University Press.

Turner, V. (1974a). Liminal to liminoid, in play, flow, and ritual: An essay in comparative symbology. In E. Norbeck & J. Buettner-Janush (Eds.), *The anthropological study of human play* (pp. 53–92). Houston: Rice University Studies.

Turner, V. (1974b). *Dramas, fields and metaphors. Symbolic action in human society.* Ithaca, NY: Cornell University Press.

Turner, V. (1975). *Revelation and divination in Ndembu ritual. Symbol, myth, and ritual.* Ithaca, NY: Cornell University Press.

Turner, V. (1981). Social dramas and stories about them. In W. J. T. Mitchell (Ed.), *On Narrative* (pp. 137–164). Chicago, IL: University of Chicago Press.

Turner, V. (1982). *From ritual to theatre: The human seriousness of play.* New York, NY: PAJ Press.

Turner, V. W. (1977). Process, system, and symbol: A new anthropological synthesis. *Daedalus, 106*(3), 61–80.

Turner, V. W., Bruner, E. M., & Geertz, C. (1986). *The anthropology of experience.* Chicago: University of Illinois Press.

Underthun, A., & Jordhus-Lier, D. C. (2018). Liminality at work in Norwegian hotels. *Tourism Geographies, 20*(1), 11–28.

US Department of Labor, & Bureau of Labor Statistics. (2018). *Occupational outlook handbook 2016–2017.* Accessed on November 8, 2018. https://www.bls.gov/ooh/.

Vallas, S. P. (1999). Rethinking post-Fordism: The meaning of workplace flexibility. *Sociological Theory, 17*(1), 68–101.

Valletta, R., & van der List, C. (2015). *Involuntary part-time work: Here to stay?* Federal Reserve Bank of San Francisco Economic Letters. Accessed on March 19, 2017. https://www.frbsf.org/economic-research/files/el2015-19.pdf.

Van Gennep, A. (1960). *The rites of passage.* London, UK: Routledge & Kegan Paul.

Vesala, H., & Tuomivaara, S. (2018). Experimenting with work practices in a liminal space: A working period in a rural archipelago. *Human Relations, 71*(10), 1371–1394.

Von Hippel, C., Mangum, S. L., Greenberger, D. B., Heneman, R. L., & Skoglind, J. D. (1997). Temporary employment: Can organizations and employees both win? *Academy of Management Perspectives, 11*(1), 93–104.

Wagner, E. L., Newell, S., & Kay, W. (2012). Enterprise systems projects: The role of liminal space in enterprise systems implementation. *Journal of Information Technology, 27*(4), 259–269.

Waldorf, G. (2016). 'Why working multiple jobs will be the new normal. *Entrepreneur*, July, 12. Retrieved January 4, 2018, from www.entrepreneur. com/article/278769

Whittington, R., Pettigrew, A., Peck, S., Fenton, E., & Conyon, M. (1999). Change and complementarities in the new competitive landscape: A European panel study, 1992–1996. *Organization Science, 10*(5), 583–600.

Wieting, S. G. (1972). Myth and symbol analysis of Claude Levi-Strauss and Victor Turner. *Social Compass, 19*(2), 139–154.

Wilhoit, E. D. (2017). 'My drive is my sacred time': Commuting as routine liminality. *Culture and Organization, 23*(4), 263–276.

Winkler, I., & Mahmood, M. K. (2015). The liminality of temporary agency work: Exploring the dimensions of Danish temporary agency workers' liminal experience. *Old Site of Nordic Journal of Working Life Studies, 5*(1), 51–68.

Wood, P. (2012). Blogs as liminal space: Student teachers at the threshold. *Technology, Pedagogy and Education, 21*(1), 85–99.

World Economic Forum. (2016). The future of jobs: Employment, skills and workforce strategy for the fourth industrial revolution. *World economic forum*, Geneva, Switzerland.

World Employment Confederation. (2016). *The future of work. White paper from the employment industry* (September).

Wright, C. (2009). Inside out? Organizational membership, ambiguity and the ambivalent identity of the internal consultant. *British Journal of Management, 20*(3), 309–322.

Wright, A. L., & Gilmore, A. (2012). Threshold concepts and conceptions: Student learning in introductory management courses. *Journal of Management Education, 36*(5), 614–635.

Yagil, D., & Medler-Liraz, H. (2013). Moments of truth: Examining transient authenticity and identity in service encounters. *Academy of Management Journal, 56*(2), 473–497.

Ybema, S., Beech, N., & Ellis, N. (2011). Transitional and perpetual liminality: An identity practice perspective. *Anthropology Southern Africa, 34*(1–2), 21–29.

Yellen, J. L. (2014). *Monetary policy and financial stability*. International Monetary Fund. Accessed on March 19, 2017. https://www.federalreserve. gov/newsevents/speech/yellen20140702a.htm.

Zabusky, S. E., & Barley, S. R. (1997). You can't be a stone if you're cement': Reevaluating the emic identities of scientists in organizations. *Research in Organizational Behavior, 19*, 361–404.

Zysman, J., & Kenney, M. (2017). Intelligent tools and digital platforms: Implications for work and employment. *Intereconomics, 52*(6), 329–334.

Index

Printed in the United States
by Baker & Taylor Publisher Services